21 PRINCIPLES FOR EFFECTIVE LIVING

DR. EDWARD D. ROBERTS, PH.D.

Outskirts Press, Inc.
Denver, Colorado

21 Principles for Effective Living
All Rights Reserved.
Copyright © 2008 Dr. Edward D. Roberts, Ph.D.
V2.0

Outskirts Press, Inc.
http://www.outskirtspress.com

ISBN: 978-1-4327-2270-8

Outskirts Press and the "OP" logo are trademarks belonging to Outskirts Press, Inc.

PRINTED IN THE UNITED STATES OF AMERICA

Acknowledgements

To my Lord and Savior, Jesus the Christ, without whom which, neither this work nor I would be possible.

To my entire family: the Roberts, the Smiths & the Sermons. I am doubly honored to be a part of our great family.

To Pastor Sharon and Pastor Ween, the "Aaron and Hur" of my life. I love and admire both of you.

To my Living Waters Ministries Worldwide Family. Thank you for your years of support, prayers and encouragement. We are on our way!

To my beloved Apostle, Dr. Paul S. Higgs and my entire K.O.K.E.M. family. Thank you for being there when no one else was.

Dedication

To the memory and legacy of my parents: the late Bishop John H. Roberts and the late Missionary Mildred E. Roberts. I thank God for all of your sacrifice, example and love. Without both of you, I am not.

To the memory and legacy of my "other Mother": the late Missionary Ruth I. Smith. I will always admire your zest for life and your dedication to Christ.

To all who are walking this challenging "Journey of Life." May this work encourage you and give you success in uncommon hours.

"Among the most noble of all pursuits lay:
the education of our children and
the provision of service to all people;
And I am endeavoring to be fully engaged in
both of these."

-Dr. Edward D. Roberts, Ph.D.
Author

Introduction

Hello, there. How are you doing? I am glad that you picked this book up to read. It has been pre-destined for both of you to meet.

I don't know if you are like me, but I want more out of life. And guess what? I want more out life for you too!

That is why I have written this book entitled *21 Principles for Effective Living, Vol. 1*. This book is based on my observations, revelations and experiences in life. I give all credit to my Creator, Jesus Christ for the information contained in this book. It gives tremendous information on: love, forgiveness, relationships, finances and divorce, to name a few. This book can be read like a novel from cover to cover. However, its true design is to serve as a *companion guide* along your life's journey. So, what do you say, let's get to work!

Let's start by defining the term *principle*. The *Merriam-Webster Online Dictionary* gives the following definitions for the term '*principle*':

> "a comprehensive and fundamental law, doctrine, or assumption **b** (1) : a rule or code of conduct(2) : habitual devotion to right principles <a man of *principle*> **c** : the laws or facts of nature underlying the working of an artificial device **2** : a primary source : **ORIGIN** **3 a** : an underlying faculty or endowment <such *principles* of human nature as greed and curiosity"

So, in short, *principles* are those underlying foundations that support both our universe and our lives. We can't change them. Nor can we corrupt them. However, we can cooperate with them. I have both noticed and observed over the years that *effective* people have many common traits. It seems that they have some special powers or insight. Maybe it's intellect. Maybe its luck. Maybe it's both. Or perhaps, they have discovered the "pillars that our universe are founded upon" and have learned how to work in cooperation with them.

Okay, now that we have a working definition for the term principle, what is the definition of *effective*? Well, again the Merriam-Webster Online Dictionary defines *effective* as:

> "the actual production of or the power
> to produce an effect [or result]."

While we are at it, we might as well define the term *living*. The Merriam-Webster Online Dictionary gives this wonderful definition of *living*:

"to have a life rich in experience."

Wow! Isn't that great? *Living* is not having the boring, unproductive life to which many of us have grown accustomed. But it means having a life chock-full o' adventures, encounters and positive results! Whew! I want that type of life! What about you?

So, to sum it all up, *21 Principles for Effective Living* are:

21 fundamental laws that will turn our lives into power-producing plants that will incite positive change in our lives and the lives of others.

It is no secret that this book is written from the Christian perspective. And this may be unattractive and repulsive to some of you. However, I say to you that these principles don't simply work for Christians. They work for anyone who recognizes them, respects them, relates to them and most of all, practices them. This book is not about religion. *It is about* relationship. *It is about* relationship *with ourselves, with each other, with our universe and with our Creator.*

Finally, my hope and prayer is that these *21 Principles for Effective Living* will challenge and enable us to look at age-old problems with new-life perspective. If at the end of this journey, we are just a little nicer to each other, just a little more patient with each other and just a bit more like our Creator, then this work shall not have been in vain.

Thank you for your interest in this project.

Table of Contents

CHAPTER 1
Relationships

"Any relationship can work, where
Love is the Boss and Forgiveness is the Secretary."

"Then there arose a reasoning among them, which of
them should be the greatest."
-Luke 9:46

I remember a story told to me by my Dad. He said that one day his brothers and himself had come upon a great idea. This idea would surely make them rich. Famous. Maybe, even both. They concocted the idea of going into business together. Their business would be a family store. Oh, how wonderful! Three brothers working together, side by side in unity. However, I must sadly report that the family business never got off the ground – it never even started. Can you guess why? I will tell you why. According to my father, the genesis of the "family business" was impeded and halted by one intriguing question. And this question has suspended the family dream for nearly a century. The question simply was, "Who is going to be the boss?" Both my father and his brothers, just like presidential candidates during election time, touted their own horn as to why they were each qualified to be "the boss." And since neither of them could persuade each other to concede to their obvious genius, the family store never became a reality.

This illustration makes one wonder, "How many great dreams, inventions and partnerships have never been realized because everyone wanted to be the boss and no one wanted to be the servant?" This was the situation with Jesus' disciples. One day the disciples had been disputing and debating about who was Jesus' greatest disciple. Each one, I'm sure, was "blowing his own horn" about why he was the prime candidate for: GREATEST DISCIPLE. Can't you just hear them now? Peter and Andrew bragging about how they were minding their business, just casting their nets into the sea, and then came along Jesus who asked them to come and work for Him? Can't you see Peter emphasizing that Jesus changed his name to Cephas, meaning 'stone?' Then we can hear James and John sharply retort that that wasn't anything to brag about. Because, the same thing happened to them also: while they were mending their nets, Jesus came and asked them to follow Him also. Not to be out-done, Phillip adds that Jesus found him and said unto him, "Follow me." Then, showing supremacy to all, Nathanael would remind everyone that he was the only discile in whom Jesus said that there wasn't any guile. On top of that, Nathanael would continue to add that Jesus gave a "prophetic word" only to him. But now arises my question, "What would happen if Love was the Boss and Forgiveness was the Secretary?"

Well, let us first define 'love.' *Love is a covenant entered into by choice and dedicated to the construction of another person, place or thing.* In other words, love is not a feeling. Actually, it is a commitment to someone or something other than ourselves. According to the Apostle Paul in I Corinthians 13, love doesn't promote itself; it promotes others.

Next, let us define 'forgiveness.' Forgiveness isn't forgetting what someone did to you. Actually, it is remembering and choosing not "to press charges." The Apostle Paul also states in I Corinthians that love doesn't "keep score." Although it remembers –that is the Secretary part- it doesn't look for opportunity to get revenge.

Therefore, I am convinced that if the "Boss" of a relationship is Love, which only seeks to construct and promote. And that if the "Secretary" of a relationship is Forgiveness, which waives the right and opportunity to "press charges." Then, that relationship which is supported and supervised by both of these nobilities will certainly meet with success in unprecedented hours.

Notice what Jesus said to His disciples that were campaigning to be the 'Greatest Disciple.' He said in Mark 9:35, "If any man desire to be first, the same shall be last of all and servant of all." And this is the complete duty of love: to serve others.

3

CHAPTER 2
Forgiveness

"Forgiveness isn't forgetting; actually, it is
remembering and choosing not to 'press charges."

"....forgive, and ye shall be forgiven; "
-Luke 6:37c

I remember a story that I heard sometime ago on a
Mississippi Mass Choir album. The preacher gave an
excellent narration about a little boy who was playing
in his backyard and pretending to be an all-star
baseball pitcher. The young lad was using everything
for a target: a tree; a bush; an old pail. Just then, the
family duck was walking across the yard. He decided
that he would see how close he could throw a stone
next to the duck's head without hitting him. The little
boy wound up and hurled the stone towards the

duck. Then all of sudden, to the young lad's sheer horror, he watched the stone smash the duck right in the head. Yes, you guessed right, the duck was dead! Both panic-stricken and afraid, the little boy immediately looked around to see if anyone saw what happened. As his little eyes scanned the yard for any witnesses, no one was to be seen for miles. Then, just as he began to breathe a sigh of relief, he heard an unpleasantly familiar voice – that of his little sister. She screamed, "Ooooh, I'm gonna tell! I'm gonna tell Momma and Dad just what you did!" Anticipating and visualizing the horrific consequences, the young boy began to plead and bargain with his sister. He even went as far as to tell her that he would do "anything" for her if she just wouldn't tell what had happened. "Anything?," replied the sister, sensing the opportunity of a lifetime. "Anything!" replied the desperate young man. Just then the sister jumped into a little red wagon and ordered her brother to pull the wagon. He had to pull her everywhere that they went: to church, to school and to the store. Then, on one particularly hot and humid day, the young boy became tired of pulling his sister around in the wagon. He begged her for a break. However, she sharply retorted, "Pull the wagon! Or else, I'm gonna tell what you did." Wearied, worn and wretched, the young boy weighed his options: continue to pull his sister around in the wagon or go to his parents and tell them what he had done to the family duck. Finally and fearfully, he decided to confront his parents. He slowly opened the rickety, old screen door and gingerly walked into the kitchen where his mother was preparing dinner. "Mom," asked the young man, "do you have a minute to talk?" "Sure, son," replied the mother. "Well, do you remember our family duck that died?" asked the son. "I sure do. What about it?" replied the mother. "Well, umm....it

6

was a mistake and I didn't mean to do it, but I accidentally threw a stone and hit the duck in the head. And that is how it died," confessed the sad, young lad. Then to his surprise, the mother said, "I know. I was standing right here, looking out the kitchen window when you did it. And I forgive you." Immediately, the young boy leapt into his mother's arms, hugging and thanking her for her forgiveness. But just then the boy remembered his father also and asked his mother, "But what about Dad?" She replied, "He forgives you, too!" Now, both overjoyed and relieved, the boy ran out the kitchen and into the yard. Just then, he heard the voice of his sister demanding that he "Pull the wagon!" The young man stuck out his chest, lifted up his head and told his sister, "Pull your own wagon! Because I have gone and got my 'duck business' straight."

Like the young man in our illustration, many people are either carrying needless burdens around in life or being needless burdens in life because of the unwillingness to forgive. I believe that this stems from a misconception of what forgiveness is and what it does. True forgiveness doesn't require a person to forget the injustices done unto them. Actually, it is relatively impossible for us to forget these infractions – or anything else for that matter. It all has to do with the way our Creator designed us. Martin Crone in *Psychology Today* gives an excellent explanation of the way human memory works. He goes on to explain that human memory is basically divided into two categories: 1) recording ; and 2) recall. When a human receives information into the brain through one of the five senses (e.g sight, taste, smell, hearing and touch) it is *permanently* recorded there. That information is then retrieved easily or difficultly, depending upon how it was stored (e.g. organized; disorganized).

It is just like looking for a book in a library. It will generally take less time to locate a specific book in library that is organized categorically, alphabetically and numerically than it would take to locate a book in room with thousands of books in disarray. This explains why we can recall certain dates, times and people more easily than others.

So what does all of this have to do with forgiveness? Well, certain 'trigger events" will recall certain information and place it in our active conscience. For example: A couple is walking down the street hand in hand –laughing and smiling. This event could recall the time when you had a partner, but that partner cheated on you. The point is that just because you *remember* that event, does not mean that you have not forgiven that person or "gotten over" that event. It simply means that your human brain is working the way it was designed to work: to remember. However, how we respond or react to this information determines if we have truly forgiven a person. If we have truly forgiven a person, even though we may remember how they offended us, we will not take any offensive action to gain revenge or equity. This is what is meant by the phrase "not press charges." Spiritually, it means that although I have a legal right to seek judgment for loss and damages caused in my life by another individual, I make a conscience choice to "drop the charges" against this individual. Why? Simply because Jesus said so!

Looking back at our illustration, neither the mother, nor the father, forgot what their son had done to the family duck. This is known because the mother replies to her son's question that she did *remember* the event. However, both the father and herself *chose* (i.e. will) not "to press charges" against their son. In

8

other words, they "gave up their legal right to seek restitution for loss and damages" for the family duck. This action both repaired and restored the family. But, it also taught the young boy about the power of forgiveness.

Dear Reader, "Have you gotten your 'duck business' straight?" Why not start today by forgiving a loved one......a foe......a friend.........yourself! I am most certain that it will make their *day* – or even their *life* for that matter!

CHAPTER 3
Divorce

"Divorce is not a commandment,
nor it is a solution: it is an option."

"[Jesus] saith unto them, Moses, because of the
hardness of your hearts, [permitted] you to put away
your wives, but from the beginning it was not so."
-Matthew 19:8 (KJV)

J. Allan Petersen gives a very powerful story about a
couple contemplating divorce. He writes:

"Newspaper columnist and minister George Crane
tells of a wife who came into his office full of ha-
tred toward her husband. "I do not only want to
get rid of him, I want to get even. Before I divorce
him, I want to hurl him as much as he has me."

11

Dr. Crane suggested an ingenious plan "Go home and act as if you really love your husband. Tell him how much he means to you. Praise him for every decent trait. Go out of your way to be as kind, considerate, and generous as possible. Spare no efforts to please him, to enjoy him. Make him believe you love him. After you've convinced him of your undying love and that you cannot live without him, then drop the bomb. Tell him that your're getting a divorce. That will really hurt him." With revenge in her eyes, she smiled and exclaimed, "Beautiful, beautiful. Will he ever be surprised!" And she did it with enthusiasm. Acting "as if." For two months she showed love, kindness, listening, giving, reinforcing, sharing. When she didn't return, Crane called. "Are you ready now to go through with the divorce?"

"Divorce?" she exclaimed. "Never! I discovered I really do love him." Her actions had changed her feelings. Motion resulted in emotion. The ability to love is established not so much by fervent promise as often repeated deeds."

Marriage is for life and therefore, shouldn't be entered into lightly. In God's sight, the bonds of marriage are sacred. However, there are many modern and mixed views that attempt to distort and destroy this view.

Let's look at the history and purpose of divorce. According to the scriptures (Deut. 24:1-4), the prophet Moses *permitted* men to give their wives a *bill of divorcement*. This bill could only be granted if the husband found some "uncleanness" in his wife. However, when this bill of divorcement is examined more closely, it can be seen that this is one of the first victories in the protection and promotion of Women's' Rights. It must be noted that certain liberties available to women today were not available to the women of Moses' day. A wife was not permitted to be gainfully employed outside of her household, nor could she earn a salary. Her total provision (i.e. financial, physical, social, etc.) would come from her husband. In time, this would prove catastrophic for a wife that no longer "found favor in her husband's eyes." Before the Mosaic bill of divorcement, husbands were simply putting their wives out of the house with nowhere to go (Mal. 2). This put the ostracized wife in a very precarious situation: she could neither remarry, nor could she obtain employment. Therefore, our God in His infinite mercy and wisdom, made provision for the wife through the bill of divorcement. With this document, the wife was allowed to remarry and thus, regain her life and her livelihood.

1. Legal vs. Spiritual

This brings us to the next aspect of divorce. Divorce is only a *legal* separation. It recognizes the permanent dissolution of the bond of matrimony. It deals with and determines the custody of children and the allocation of assets: money, property, etc.

However, what divorce doesn't deal with is the *spiritual* aspect of separation. Like it or not, believe it or not, when two people have co-habitated and copulated for any given length of time, there is a spiritual connection there. It can be good or it can be bad. However, it is most important to know and admit that the bond exists. The Apostle Paul deals with this very concept in the book of I Corinthians 7:14-17. He informs his readers that a man and a harlot that have sexual intercourse become "one flesh (i.e. person)." It is noteworthy here to look at the history of the Jewish wedding. It was not like our modern-day matrimonial services presided over by civic officials or clergy. No, it was actually presided over by family members of the bride and the groom. Today's marriage is made "official" when a qualified civic official or clergy member asks the bride and groom to affirm their vows to each other. Once this happens, this official pronounces the couple as "husband and wife." However, the Jews employed totally different means to declare a marriage "official." The first pre-requisite of the bride was that she be a virgin. This was very important in declaring the marriage official, as we shall see. Next, the bride and groom would be favored with speeches and well wishes from family and friends. Then would come the moment of truth. The bride and groom were required to enter the bridal tent and to "consummate their marriage." In other words, the marriage couple had to engage in sexual intercourse while family and friends waited outside. Well, for what were the family and friends waiting? They were waiting for the marriage cloth. This cloth was placed under the bride during the act of copulation. If indeed she were a virgin, this cloth would become stained with her blood. So, once the couple finished their "consummation" they would rush to the tent door and hold up the cloth. If it were stained with the bride's blood, then there was great rejoicing and celebration. But if the cloth were not stained with the bride's blood, then it meant almost certain death for that bride. Therefore, we see that what made the Jewish marriage "official" was the sexual intercourse, not the reciting of vows. According to this view, it is sexual intercourse that joins two individuals together spiritually.

So, if sexual intercourse joins two individuals spiritually, what *divides* them spiritually? Well, let us first examine

14

our human make-up. One popular view holds that humans are tri-partite beings. That simply means that we are made up of three (3) parts: body, soul and spirit. Without getting too theological, my summation is this: the body does; the soul determines; and the spirit knows. In short, the body is basically a "puppet" that carries out the desires and wishes of the soul. The spirit on the other hand is our "knowledge and moral base." It advises and makes recommendations to the soul on what is right and what is wrong. And the soul, which is the "seat" or "center" of our emotions, determines whether or not it follow the advice of the spirit. The soul is the 'cauldron' that boils with our love and our passions; our desires and dislikes; our fantasies and our fears. It is to our soul that another being becomes attached. Hence, the terms "soul-mates" and "soul ties." It is these soul ties with soul mates that must be severed also, if a divorce is to be effective and final. But who or what do we know that is able to destroy something that we can definitely feel, but certainly cannot see. Well, in the book of Hebrews, chapter 4 and verse 12, it says, "For the word of God is living and active. Sharper than any double-edged sword, it penetrates even to **dividing soul and spirit**, joints and marrow; it judges the thoughts and attitude of the heart. (NIV)" It is the Word of God (i.e. Truth) that divides (i.e. cuts, severs) soul and spirit. So simply stated, "The truth shall make you free." The truth about yourself, your spouse, your-ex, etc. and the acknowledgement and acceptance of it will perform the "spiritual" separation.

Unfortunately, although marriage is designed to last for life, there may come a time when divorce is inevitable. This is not because the marriage is unsalvageable. It is because the marriage partners have chosen not to salvage it through prayer, compromise and sacrifice.

15

CHAPTER 4
Trouble

"It is better to stay as far away from trouble
as one can, than to see how close
one can get to it without falling into it."

"Abram dwelt in the land of Canaan, and Lot dwelt
in the cities of the plain, and pitched his tent toward
Sodom. But the men of Sodom were wicked and
sinners before the Lord exceedingly."
-Genesis 13:12-13 (KJV)

My father, the late Bishop John H. Roberts, once told
me a story about a rich man that needed to hire a
chauffeur. So, he posted an ad in the local newspaper. Two prospective applicants replied to the ad
and showed up for the interview. The rich man then
explained to these two gentlemen that they would

be required to take him on a test drive along a pre-scribed route. He warned both of these drivers that there was a humungous pothole at a certain point along the test route. So, as the story goes, Applicant# 1 jumped in behind the steering wheel and took off with his potential employer in the back seat. He drove along the course and saw the pothole in the road. Sure to please his soon-to-be boss and to show his superior driving skills, Applicant# 1 drove as close to the pothole in the road as he could without falling into it. Actually, I'm told, he drove so close to it that he knocked off gravel and rocks into this hole. He then completed his course and it was now turn for Applicant# 2 to drive. Applicant #2 drove the rich man along the test course and came upon the dreaded pothole. However, as he approached this crater in the road, he drove as far away from it as he could. This applicant completed his course and returned to hear the results. The rich man informed both applicants that he had decided to hire Applicant# 2 as his chauffeur. He then gave the reason for his decision. He said that he didn't want to hire a person that shows how close they can get to trouble without falling into it. However, he stated that he wanted to hire a person that stayed as far away from trouble as they could!

This principle is excellently illustrated in the story of Abraham and Lot. In Genesis 13 Abraham and Lot are both rich with livestock and servants. They are so rich that there isn't enough land for them to dwell together. Their herdsmen are constantly getting into altercations and fights over grazing areas for the animals. Abraham is aware of the situation and makes a proposal to Lot. He begins by stating that they are family and that this type of situation shouldn't exist between them. Therefore, he asks Lot to choose what part of the land that he wants for his livestock, herdsmen and family. If he chooses the eastern part, then Abraham will choose the western part. And if Lot were to choose the western part, then Abraham would choose the eastern. Lot chose the beautiful Jordan Valley to the east of them. He went there with his flocks and servants, and thus, parted company with Abraham. For Abraham stayed in the land of Canaan, while Lot lived among the cities of the plain, settling at a place near the city of Sodom. One should note, the men of this area were unusually wicked and sinned greatly against Jehovah.

While Lot lived in this area, a war broke out. Unfortunately, Lot and all that he owned was taken captive by enemy forces. On another occasion, two angels warned Lot to leave the city with his wife and daughters because God was getting ready to destroy it along with Gomorroah because of its wickedness. Then, during the escape, Lot's wife turned into a "pillar of salt." Shortly, thereafter, Lot became drunk and committed incest with his daughters. And both of these daughters bore him sons: Moab and Bennammi (Genesis 20:38).

Thus, we can learn from Lot's life that being too close to trouble can result in getting into trouble. Lot experienced the following troubles by simply moving too close to trouble: kidnapping; attempted rape; death of wife; incest with his daughters; "father" of his grandchildren!

Therefore, the recommendation is to stay as far away from trouble as one can.

CHAPTER 5
Love

"Love is not a feeling: it is a <u>covenant</u> entered into by <u>choice</u>, solely <u>committed</u> to the <u>construction</u> of a person, place or thing."

"This is my commandment, That ye love
one another, as I have loved you."
                              -John 15:12 (KJV)

An inspiring excerpt appears in an edition of
Our Daily Bread. It reads:

"In his book <u>Mere Christianity</u>, C.S. Lewis wrote, "Do not waste your time bothering whether you 'love' your neighbor. Act as if you did. As soon as we do this, we find one of the great secrets. When you are behaving as if you loved someone, you will presently come to love him. If you injure someone you dislike, you will find yourself disliking him more. If you do him a good turn, you will find yourself disliking him less."

I remember one occasion when I asked God to help me love more like Him. He replied with a quick, emphatic and resounding, "No!" I was devastated. Here was this big, gigantic –supposed- "God of Love' who wouldn't help me to love, too. Well, after I calmed down, the Lord explained it all to me. He explained that I already had all of the love in the world inside of me. And that all I had to do was to make a choice to release it through action. He went on further and showed me a hideous picture of myself. He showed me that when people were nice to me that I *chose* to be nice (i.e. love) to them. However, when people were not nice to me I chose *not* to be nice (i.e. love) to them. Whew! What an ugly picture! Furthermore, Jesus told His disciples that if they hated their enemies and loved only their friends, that they were not any better than the publicans (Matthew 5:43-46).

Many people define love as a feeling of bliss, joy and happiness. In the opinion of this author, nothing could be farther from the truth. It is my estimation that there are four components of love:

1) choice;
2) covenant;
3) commitment; and
4) construction. Let's look at each of these in further detail.

22

1. Choice

Love is a result of choice. It is subject always to the decision-making power of the human will. If the will says, "No," then love will not be released. And it must remain as a prisoner of the human heart -no matter how powerful it is. On the other hand, if the human will says, "Yes," then love will be released.

This protocol and order is demonstrated in the three branches of the United States Government: legislative; judicial; and executive. Regarding all United States laws that govern its people, each branch of our government performs a different function. The legislative branch *makes* the laws. The judicial branch decides which laws are constitutional. And the executive branch *enforces* the laws.

Likewise, our spirit/mind (i.e. legislative branch) makes the law. Our soul/will (i.e. judicial branch) decides the law (i.e. whether to love or not). And our body (i.e. executive branch) enforces or carries out 'the law' to love or not to love.

2. Covenant

Love is a covenant or agreement between two or more parties. Where there is no agreement love cannot exist.

A covenant is equivalent to a contract. Some of the items that a contract contains are:

- The names and signatures of all parties involved.
- The date of the agreement.

- The promises made by each party to uphold the contract.
- The terms/timeline of the contract.
- The penalties that will be assessed if either party fails to comply with the contract.

Likewise, whether written or implied, there are persons, promises, payments and penalties involved with the "Contract of Love."

3. Commitment

Commitment is the dedication and diligence in upholding the terms of the contract.

Commitment is the quality that makes love paramount to all other virtues. Where there is commitment there are no excuses, infidelity, unfaithfulness or unreliability.

Commitment is just like the sun: whether the sky is cloudy or clear..........it rises everyday!

Likewise, where true love exists, there is commitment. And where there is commitment there is continuity, reliability and security.

4. Construction

Construction is the trademark and tell-tell sign of true love. Anywhere that love exists there is construction taking place.

Construction is the justification for love. It is the payoff, the reason for choosing and committing to the "Contract of Love."

The goal and sole intent of love is: to construct and build up a person, place or thing to a glory greater than that of its former self. Love never destroys. And it never deceives.

5. Hypothesis

If this author's definition of love is correct, then it must be in harmony with the most renowned "love scripture" of all time: John 3:16. It states:

> "For God so loved the world, that he gave his only begotten Son, that whosoever believeth in him should not perish, but have everlasting life."

a. Choice

In this verse God makes a voluntary choice to love the world. No scriptures before or after show that the world asked God to love it. God saw that it needed help and chose to love it.

b. Covenant

The parties involved are God, His Son, Jesus Christ and the World. The provision of the contract is three-fold:

1. God gives His only Son as a sacrifice to atone for the sins of the world.

2. God cancels the death sentence pronounced on the world (i.e. "...should not perish").

3. God gives everlasting life to the world.

The obligation of the treaty is simple:

The world/individual must believe in Jesus, the only begotten Son of God in order to escape death and received everlasting life.

c. Commitment

God the Father is committed to His creation. When the world was in its deepest need, He did not abandon it nor destroy it ("For God so loved the world…"). He developed a strategy to revitalize and resurrect it.

d. Construction

God the Father made a provision for the world's inhabitants to "upgrade their membership." Under this new provision all humans can escape destruction (i.e. perish) and enjoy construction (i.e. everlasting life).

In summation: love is simply doing what we can do to improve the lives of others.

CHAPTER 6
Recovery

"Two things precede recovery:
inventory and discovery."

"But as one of them was chopping, his ax head fell
into the river. "Ah, my lord!" he cried.
"It was a borrowed ax!"

-II Kings 6:5

NBCSanDiego.com featured the following
article about a man reunited with his stolen
Corvette after 37 years:

"A Southern California man was reunited with his
prized Corvette Tuesday -- 37 years after thieves
drove off with it. Alan Poster's 1968 Corvette was

stolen in New York City in 1969. A collector in Long Beach was selling the car overseas when customs agents called New York police. Officials tracked down Poster in California.

'It is definitely a miracle,' Poster said. 'In speaking to the police, the odds of them finding me were a million to one; it's a ridiculous number. Why this came to me is a miracle.' Poster does not know where the car has been all these years."

At one time or another many of us have lost somethingof great value. Maybe it was a cell phone,some expensive jewelry, a wallet or a purse. Whatis even worse is when the item that you lose doesnot belong to you. In either instance, the loss canbe quite nerve-wracking.

A similar incident appears in the book of II Kings chapter 6. A group of 'seminary' students are living in cramped dormitory space. Afterwards, they come up with the brilliant and industrious idea to build a larger dormitory. These students propose this idea to their 'professor,' Elisha, and obtain his approval. In addition, the students invite their beloved teacher to come down to the Jordan River to view this construction project. Notably, one student begins to cut down a tree for lumber. As he swings his axe handle towards the tree he makes a startling discovery: there is no axe head on the end! It is at that moment that he notices the axe head falling and sinking into the river. He cries out intently to his professor for help. His teacher asks him what is the problem. The student then explains the situation. Elisha asks the student to show him the location at which the axe head fell into the water. The student points to the location and the teacher throws a stick into the water at the same location. Amazingly, the iron axe head floats to the surface of the water and the student recovers it. Wow, what a story!

Three steps took place in order for the student to reclaim the lost axe head: inventory, discovery and recovery. Let's examine what occurred in each step.

1. Inventory

In our story the student is hard at work cutting down trees with an axe. We don't know how many trees he had already cut down before losing the axe head. But we are sure that he suspended all chopping down of trees until he found the lost axe head. There is one important question that we should ask ourselves: "How did the student know that he had lost the axe head? Perhaps, it was when the axe handle made contact with the tree and sent shockwaves up through the arms of the student. Or maybe it was when the student kept swinging the handle at the tree, but the tree never fell. I believe that the student decided to inspect (i.e. take inventory) of the axe because it wasn't cutting down the tree, despite his constant swinging. This illustration is comparable to pushing a vacuum cleaner across the carpet and noticing that it isn't picking up the dirt. You are inclined to turn off the power to the vacuum cleaner and inspect it for blockage or malfunction.

Likewise, the first step in recovery is taking inventory. In other words, taking inventory means finding out "what I have on hand." The *Merriam-Webster Dictionary* defines *inventory* as:

"an itemized list of current assets: as (1) : a catalog of the property of an individual or estate (2) : a list of goods on hand"

Think about it. Would you begin to look for something that you thought you had? For example, you may think that your new Mercedes-Benz is parked safely in your garage. With that thought, would you call the police or your insurance company? No, because you think that you have it. But what if you go to your garage to see your car (i.e. take inventory) and God forbid, it isn't in your garage? What course of action would you take? You would probably call the police and your insurance company in an effort to recover your property.

The point is this: we don't look for things that we think we already have. And this is the reason that many of us don't recover our rightful property (examples: joy, health, prosperity). We think that we have it, when the sad reality is that it is lost or misplaced.

2. Discovery

Once the seminary student takes inventory of the axe he makes an alarming discovery about the axe: it is missing the axe head. The student cries out, "Alas...!" It is very important to understand this term *alas*. According to the *Merriam-Webster Dictionary* it is: *used to express unhappiness, pity, or concern.* Likewise, it is easy to become unhappy when we discover that we don't have what we think we have.

The root word of *discovery* is *discover*. The *Merriam-Webster Dictionary* defines *discover* as:

1 a : to make known or visible **: <u>EXPOSE</u> b** *archaic* **:
<u>DISPLAY</u>
2 a :** to obtain sight or knowledge of for the first time **: <u>FIND</u>** <*discover* the solution> **b : <u>FIND OUT</u>** <*discovered* he was out of gas>

Therefore, in its truest sense of the word, when a *discovery* has been made that something of ours is lost, it is the FIRST TIME that we have knowledge of this loss. And this knowledge is so key and so critical. The reason is that it will prompt us to begin a search to recover our goods.

3. Recovery

Once the seminary student has discovered that the axe head was missing he immediately launched a plan of recovery. By the term *recover* we mean *"to get back" (Merriam-Webster Dictionary).*

Firstly, he notifies the person that can rectify the situation. He cries out, "Alas, *Master!*" Notice that he didn't tell the other seminarians. Nor did he keep it to himself. He went to the one whom he knew could remedy the situation: his Master. Similarly, it is necessary for us to partner and align with individuals and agencies that can help us to recover our "stuff."

Secondly, the student is able to give a detailed description of what was lost and where it was last seen. This may seem like simple information, but it can be very valuable in the midst of a crisis to recover lost goods. Likewise, we need to be specific about what we are attempting to recover. And also, we need to be cooperative and supportive with those who are aiding us in our recovery.

Thirdly, the student was responsible to go and retrieve the axe head. Remember, the student had shown his teacher the place where the axe head had fallen into the water. And then the teacher threw a stick into the water at that same location. Following this, the axe head begins to float on top of the water. What happened next is most noteworthy. The teacher instructs the student to go and retrieve the floating axe head (II Kings 6:7). In the same manner, we must take the primary responsibility in recovering our property. Although individuals and/or agencies may *assist* us in our recovery process, ultimately we are the ones that are required to go and retrieve our "floating axe head."

In summation, "there are two things that precede recovery: inventory and discovery."

CHAPTER 7
Understanding

"Give a foolish person a shovel and they
will start digging. Give a wise person a shovel and
they will ask, "What do you want me to do with it?"

"...and with all thy getting get understanding."
                                                    -Proverbs 4:7

There is a story about a son that wanted to give his mother an unforgettable gift. He read of a bird that had a vocabulary of thousands of words, could speak in numerous languages and could even recite Bible verses. He paid upwards of $50,000 for the bird and had it delivered to his Mom. The next day, anxious to hear his mother's reaction, the son telephoned her. When she picked up the phone he asked his mother, "How was the bird?" And she replied, "It was delicious!"

In this humorous story, the mother used the bird for

nourishment. However, I am sure that this was not the intended use by the sender. Likewise, we have received gifts and opportunities during our lifetimes. And, more than likely, we are not using them the way the Sender has intended. Let's take a look at a few.

1. Life

The one thing that is most precious to all living beings is: life. Without it none of us would exist. It is a gift given to us at the time of our birth and retrieved at the time of our passing.

And just like the mother in the illustration, a great price was paid by the Son in order for us to receive this life. Therefore, it behooves us to ask the Giver of our gift of life, "What is this gift?" and "How do I use this gift?"

This gift of life is not to be used selfishly for our own personal gain. Nor is it to be wasted with careless and riotous living. This gift is to be used to help and improve the lives of others.

2. Health

I remember my father telling me, "Eddie, when you can eat a good meal and enjoy it, you are blessed! When you can lay down and get a good night's sleep, you are blessed! And when you can get up and bathe yourself, you are blessed!"

Dad has since passed on, but these words often replay in my mind. He was absolutely right. Everyone doesn't have good health. So those of us who have it should appreciate hit and preserve it as much as we can through proper diet, exercise and rest.

3. Family

The family is the basic building block of society. And it is the foundation of any person's life. Whether functional or dysfunctional, this social unit provides great influence on our lives to varying degrees.

Many will probably agree on this point: that an "Instruction Manual on How to Get Along with Your Family" definitely needs to be written. For those fortunate enough to have an *appearance* and semblance of a family, please consider this advice: endeavor to be a part of the solution and not a part of the commotion.

I know firsthand that it isn't always easy to get along with family members. But, I know this, also: the family that we have is the only family that we will ever have. So, I think it wise to appreciate who and what we have while we have it.

4. Time

By nature, I am a daydreamer. I can, without effort, waste untold amounts of time in dreamland. In addition, I procrastinate and put off projects (i.e. like this book) until the last and final moment.

Why am I so candid and open about my poor time management skills? Because I know that I am in good company. Stephen Covey details a quadrant exercise in his book *The Seven Habits of Highly Effective People*. This quadrant is simply a square sub-divided into four smaller squares. He labels these smaller squares: Quadrant #1, Quadrant #2, Quadrant #3 and Quadrant #4. Into Quadrant #1 he places all of our daily tasks: go to work/school, take kids to school, pick up clothes from cleaners, feed the dog, etc. Into Quadrant #2 he places our goals, the things that we really need to and want to accomplish: lose weight; complete novel; enroll into school; make career change, etc. Mr. Covey goes on to explain that we spend so much of our time on Quadrant #1 activities that we never accomplish the real goals of Quadrant #2.

Thus, our time should be consumed upon completing meaningful goals and not upon meaningless tasks.

5. Youth

Ah, blessed youth. These can be some of the most glorious years of one's life. I remember the magic of my youth: endless summer days of playing baseball, going to the movies and spending my parents' money (big smile)! The biggest responsibilities that I had at that time were: going to school, completing my homework and doing household chores. My days and nights were filled with friends and fun, hopes and dreams and the greatest deception of youth: that it will last forever.

Youth is a blessing when it is spent in the proper way. It is a time of preparation for adulthood. It is a time to be used wisely and cherished perpetually. This is a time when one plants their seeds for the future. Actions committed during this period –whether positive or negative- can follow a person for the rest of their life.

6. Money

My Dad always used to say, "It isn't how much money you make that counts; but its how much you save that counts." And over the years I have found this to be true –usually around tax time (smile). When you look at how much you made and how much you have left, you can feel like you have been robbed. Where did all of that money go? Without a written budget it is difficult to tell.

I remember when my budget was $50 per week. Can you believe it? Fifty dollars! And I couldn't wait until the day that I would make $500 per week. Well, eventually that day came and I was making much more than $500 per week. And I lived happily ever after, right? Wrong. The truth was that I did more with that $50 per week than I did with that $500 per week. What happened? Well, I succumbed to one of the oldest human trends: the more we make, the more we tend to spend. If I had continued to manage that $500 plus per week like I had managed that $50 per week, then my finances would have been in great shape. I have to agree with Dad, "It isn't how much you make that matters; but its how much you save that counts."

These are just a few of the blessings that we are granted in life. And now that we are aware that we may have some of these, lets be a little more careful in how we use them. It has been said that, "Our talents are gifts from God. And what we do with these talents are our gifts back to Him." Be blessed!

CHAPTER 8
Discipline

"Discipline is training in how we should live,
in despite of how we may feel."

"All athletes practice strict self-control...I discipline my
body like an athlete, training it to do what it should."
-I Corinthians 9:25a,27a

Author David Branon presents an insightful story in an
edition of *Our Daily Bread.* He writes:

> "When my son began his sophomore year of high
> school, he also began his second year of cross-
> country running. Steve started the year fighting for a
> spot on the varsity team, which was not an easy task.
> It meant running miles and miles and miles. It

meant lifting weights. It meant getting extra rest and eating right (well, some of the time). And it meant running his heart out at races.

His times gradually improved. Then he pulled a muscle and had to start over. But he didn't quit. Finally he gained a spot on the varsity. And by the time they ran in the regional meet, he was the third fastest runner on the team."

I remember my days of running high school track. I was a member of the varsity indoor and outdoor track teams. However, my coach required me to practice with the cross-country team during the fall. I totally despised this, since I competed in the 200m and 400m events. In addition, I continued running and practicing during the summer months. But all of this paid off during my senior year. My sprint medley relay team captured the state championship at Princeton University. In retrospect, I believe that submitting to my coach's discipline enabled me to reach this lofty goal. Likewise, I believe that any person that submits to a course of discipline will accomplish great goals.

And this is the point of discussion: submitting to a plan of discipline in order to reach a personal goal. I have divided this plan into three (3) major components: 1) The Principle; 2) The Price; and 3) The Prize. Let's examine the first component: The Principle.

1. The Principle

As a senior on the varsity track team I had one goal in mind for that year: to win the state championship.

Did you catch that word? I said, "I had a *goal*." I believe that it was the Spirit that kept "nagging" me at the beginning of this year to write down my personal goals. However, instead of obeying this prompting I continued to complete daily *tasks*. This was good. But it wasn't fulfilling. At the end of the day I was tired, but I still sensed that I hadn't accomplished anything. And if that were not bad enough, I realized that I was helping others reach their goals while ignoring my own. How could this happen? It happened because I did not identify, did not set and did not write down my goals. And just like a ship without an anchor or a leaf in the wind, I allowed myself to drift into and get blown around with other individual's goals. You see, by identifying, setting and writing down your goals you add a whole new dimension to your life! You now have purpose, a plan and a timeline. Writer David Branon goes on to say in his article:

"Having goals in life can give us the purpose and drive to accomplish something truly valuable. This principle is especially helpful in our lives as believers in Christ."

So, discipline causes us to set a goal and to develop a plan to reach it. This is the first component of discipline. Your goal may be to lose weight, to get married or purchase a new car. Whatever it is, it will start with setting your goal!

Writing down your goal(s) and doing what it takes to reach it/them are two totally different worlds. Which leads me to the second component of discipline: The Price.

41

2. The Price

Many people don't reach their goals. This isn't because they are less talented, less intelligent or have less money. It is because they are not willing to pay "the price of discipline." I remember my Dad telling me many times, "Son, anything in life worth something has a great price tag attached to it. So don't look for something for nothing." The price of discipline comes in many forms. At times the price is time away from loved ones or missing important family events. Sometimes the price is lack of much needed sleep. Or it can be rising early every morning while the whole world is still asleep. It can come in the form of excruciating, physical pain and sore muscles. Or it can simply be eating a piece of fruit instead of that double-decker, double-delicious, double-brownie sundae.

That's right, the only difference between the successful and unsuccessful person is the price that each is willing to pay. Booker T. Washington, the founder of the Tuskegee Institute, says it this way:

> "Success is to be measured not so much by the position that one has reached in life as by the obstacles which [one] has overcome."

Simply stated, "*Discipline* demands that its price be paid in full before it grants access to *The Prize*." This leads to the final component of discipline: The Prize.

3. The Prize

As fore stated, the purpose of submitting to a plan of discipline is to obtain a desired goal (i.e. the prize). In our opening illustration that prize was a place on the varsity track team. In my personal example it was winning the state championship. In your life only you can determine what you want your prize to be.

The prize is the payoff for all of the planning, hard work and diligence that an individual has paid. It is the justification for the aggravation. It is end of the means. Paraphrasing one author, "Success doesn't occur by accident. It is a planned event."

The Apostle Paul encourages us to live our lives (i.e. run) in such a way that we will win and obtain the prize (I Corinthians 9:24). In that same spirit, I am encouraging you the reader to submit to a plan of discipline that will help you reach all of your goals in life!

CHAPTER 9
Persistence

"There are no straight rivers."

The rivers run into the sea, but the sea is never full.
Then the water returns again to the rivers
and flows again to the sea.

-Ecclesiastes 1:7

I was fortunate to attend an excellent college pre-
paratory school for young men: Seton Hall Prepara-
tory, now located in West Orange, NJ. The dress
code demanded dress shoes, dress slacks, dress shirt
and tie. In addition, each student had to wear a sin-
gle-breasted blazer. Embroidered on the left breast
pocket of this blazer was the school's emblazon or
crest. I fondly remember the three Latin words that
ran across the lower part of this insignia: *Hazard zet*

45

Forward. This was a Latin phrase that meant: *"In spite of all hazards, go forward."* I have since outgrown that blazer, but I have not outgrown that teaching: to go forward, even when you run into life's obstacles.

If you take a look at rivers on a map you will notice something remarkable: there are no straight rivers! Under a magnifying glass you will notice that each one curves a little to right and little to the left. It continues to do this until it reaches its final destination: the sea.

Why do rivers do this? Is this a mistake in nature? What is going on? An attempt will be made to answer these questions. And furthermore, an attempt will be made to show how these lessons can be applied to our lives.

1. Our Path

The final destination of all rivers is ultimately the sea. This can take place in one of several ways. Many rivers start out as tiny, microscopic droplets of water that evaporate from the sea. These molecules then gather and form clouds. The clouds then release these molecules in the form of precipitation (i.e. rain, snow, ice). Much of this rain starts its journey from the mountaintops, flows down through the valley and ultimately into the sea. This is a brief description of what is termed the hydrological or water cycle. Regarding the hydrological cycle, UNESCO.org (United Nations Educational, Scientific and Cultural Organization) states:

"Solar heat evaporates water into the air from the Earth's surface. Land, lakes, rivers and oceans send up a steady stream of water vapour; this

spreads over the surface of the planet before falling down again as precipitation. Precipitation falling on land is the main source of the formation of
the waters found on land: rivers, lakes, groundwater, glaciers. A portion of atmospheric precipitation evaporates, some of it penetrates and
charges groundwater, while the rest - as river flow
- returns to the oceans where it evaporates: this
process repeats again and again. A considerable
portion of river flow does not reach the ocean,
having evaporated in the endorheic regions,
those areas with no natural surface runoff chan-
nels. On the other hand, some groundwater by-
passes river systems altogether and goes directly
to the ocean or evaporates... Water is in permanent motion, constantly changing from liquid to
solid or gaseous phase, and back again."

Two observations can be made here. First observation: nature has designed a **path** for all water molecules to travel by. Second observation: water is very
dynamic. Along its path it is constantly **changing**
from one state to another: liquid, gas and solid.

Just as a path has been provided for the water mole-
cule, a path has also been provided for humans. It is
called: *the life cycle*. Humans are conceived and
born. We then pass through four basic stages of life:
1) infancy; 2) childhood; 3) youth; and 4) adulthood.
While the classification and taxonomy may vary by
writer and/or discipline, these are the basic stages of
human life. This is "the path of life" that each human
is designed to walk through.

It has been stated that water is very dynamic: it is
constantly changing from one form to another. Like-

wise, humans are constantly growing, evolving and adapting. It is required along this path of life that we change, grow and most importantly, mature. And believe it or not, this is where many have great difficulty. Because there is one thing that humans hate more than anything else and that is: *change*.

According to Maslov's Hierarchy of Needs, one of the most basic human needs is security. And most often we find that security in constancy. In many instances, we like having the same friends, living in the same house and working for the same employer. However, the reality is that life, like water, is dynamic. It is constantly changing. It is always in motion. And if we are going to be successful then we will have to "go with the flow." Moving from one stage of life to the next can be daunting. Ask the child who is attending their first day of school or the teenager who has just left home for the first time in their life. Ask the employee who is forced to look for another job after 30 years of faithful service or the senior citizen that has to take up residence in an assisted-living community. These are just a few examples of life's changes. And as difficult as they may be, we must learn to adjust with them if we want to live effectively.

2. Our Power

Our planet Earth is populated with some of the most magnificent rivers. There is the mighty Mississippi River, the life-supporting Nile River and there is the historic Jordan River, just to name a few. But, have you have ever wondered, "Where do these rivers get their power from?"

Well, at least four (4) forces of nature contribute to

the power of all rivers: 1) The sun; 2) The wind; 3) gravity; and 4) affinity.

a. The Sun

In the first stage of our hydrological or water cycle, we mentioned that water from the oceans, seas and rivers evaporate into the air. This evaporation is possible because of the energy of the sun. When heat rays from the sun come into contact with the surface of water, the water molecules heat up and are released into the air.

I have had the privilege many times to be in the presence of great thinking and motivating people. And while they spoke or entertained, it was as if "the sun" of their personality warmed the stagnant "sea of my mind." The result was that my thoughts, like the water molecules, were released and lifted to higher state of consciousness. It is important to surround yourself with positive speaking and acting people. They can prove to be an indispensable resource in your life.

b. The Wind

After the water molecules evaporate into the atmosphere, they form into what we call *clouds*. And it is the wind that moves these clouds across the earth's atmosphere. It moves them to the majestic mountaintops where they can release their life-giving rains. It moves them across the open fields where they water the crops. It moves them across the arid and scorched desert to bring life back again.

Also, the wind blows upon the oceans and rivers. This

action results in trade winds and currents.

Likewise, just as the wind causes the clouds, rivers and oceans to come to the place where they can do the most good, I see supportive family, friends and investors as 'the wind in the sails of our lives." No matter how talented and gifted we may be, if we don't have someone to support us and help us get to where we need to be, then we may never see all that we could be. In light of this discussion, I am reminded of the song "Wind Beneath My Wings" performed by Bette Midler and written by Larry Hinley and Jeff Silbar. I believe that these lyrics perfectly honor the value of those who support us:

"Ohhhh, oh, oh, oh, ohhh.
It must have been cold there in my shadow,
To never have sunlight on your face.
You were content to let me shine, that's your way.
You always walked a step behind.

So I was the one with all the glory,
While you were the one with all the strain.
A beautiful face without a name for so long.
A beautiful smile to hide the pain.

Did you ever know that you're my hero,
And everything I would like to be?
I can fly higher than an eagle,
For you are the wind beneath my wings.

It might have appeared to go unnoticed,
But I've got it all here in my heart.
I want you to know I know the truth, of course I
     know it.
I would be nothing without you.

[Repeat Chorus]

Fly, fly, fly high against the sky,
So high I almost touch the sky.
Thank you, thank you,
Thank God for you, the wind beneath my wings.

c. Gravity

What makes rivers run down mountains and into the sea? Why, gravity, of course. This invisible force of nature reaches from within the depths of the earth out into the earth's atmosphere. It pulls at all things. Nothing and nobody is exempt. This powerful force is what gives the river its tenacity and determination to reach the sea. Even when the river encounters an obstacle (e.g. boulder, rock or tree) it won't stop flowing. It will just find an easier way to get to its goal (i.e. the sea). Science calls this "*the path of least resistance.*" The river wisely conserves its energy for "more meaningful pursuits" when it runs into an impasse. I have even seen rivers and streams turn back upon themselves 180 degrees in order to develop an "alternate and more efficient route" to reach its final destination. It seems that this trait –the path of least resistance- is inherent throughout nature. For example, lions and other predators hunt the weakest and easiest prey in order to conserve energy. These predators will hunt at night instead of during the scorching day. Again, they do this to conserve energy.

Gravity pulls the river from the mountain to the sea and keeps it "grounded." Likewise, I believe that good principles keep us grounded and motivated to reach noteworthy and noble goals. Individuals that have accomplished great feats "pull" us toward the "sea of our destiny." Without this force pulling and tugging at us we may become content to rest or stop at the hazard in our path. But good principles, good people and a Good God won't let us remain content with defeat.

d. Affinity

Water cleanses, nourishes and replenishes. However, besides these wonderful qualities, water has another additional property that distinguishes it from all other substances. Water molecules have a high affinity for one another. Another term for this is 'hydrophilia.' Simply stated, water molecules are attracted to each other. Under normal circumstances and without any external forces involved (e.g. heat) water molecules will come together and stay together.

Imagine walking outside and one drop of water falls on you. You might not even notice it. Now imagine 1,000 gallons of water falling on you. You would definitely notice that! Why? Simply, because millions up millions of tiny, microscopic water molecules decide to join forces. They decided to unite and carry out a purpose collectively that they could not have accomplished individually.

Likewise, no matter how great we are as individuals, none of us can accomplish as much by ourselves as we can with each other. That is why I believe that one of the greatest inventions of all time is: the team. You can't improve upon it. Where else in nature can you take tiny, insignificant beings and accomplish great and admirable feats? As one person told me before, "It takes teamwork to make the dream work!"

3. Our Purpose

There is a purpose for the river to reach to sea. It is a purpose that I think is amongst the noblest of all pursuits. That purpose is simply: to nourish and support everything that it touches on its way to the sea. Some of the most fertile regions on earth are those along riverbanks and waterways. It is here where fauna and flora thrive. Animal and plant life are most abundant here. Why? There is plenty of growth here because there is nourishment and sustenance here. The "Eagle-Eyed" Prophet, Isaiah, attests to this fact in the book of Isaiah 55:10,11:

"For as the rain cometh down, and the snow from heaven, and returneth not thither, but watereth the earth, and maketh it bring forth and bud, that it may give seed to the sower, and bread to the eater:

"So shall my word be that goeth forth out of my mouth: it shall not return unto me void, but it shall accomplish that which I please, and it shall prosper in the thing whereto I sent it. "

Thus, I believe that the ultimate purpose of our living is to positively affect and nourish every soul that we encounter on our path of life. Even though we each are trying to reach our own "sea of our destiny," we must – I repeat – we must help one another. I believe then that our Creator –like any good parent- will be most proud of us when He sees how we love and support one another!

CHAPTER 10
Work

"Between inspiration and manifestation lays perspiration."

"Lazy people want much but get little, but those who work hard will prosper and be satisfied."
-Proverbs 13:4

One of the greatest inventors of all times is Thomas A. Edison. He held over 1300 U.S. and foreign patents. But, his crowning achievement was the invention of the incandescent light bulb in 1879. This invention revolutionized the world and the way we live. However, this invention wasn't manifested overnight. It took a lot of work, sweat and perspiration. The following quote by Mr. Edison appeared in the 1932 edition of *Harper's Monthly*:

"Genius is one per cent inspiration, ninety-nine per cent perspiration."

Many goals are never achieved and many dreams are never realized because there is work (i.e. perspiration) involved. Our dreams and ideas must be coupled with work in order to come to fruition. Otherwise, they will remain just that: dreams and ideas.

As a point of interest, do you know that you can't copyright and idea? I found this out recently while registering a work with the United States Copyright Office. In order to receive a copyright for an idea, that idea must be put into a fixed format (hint: work) such as an article, book or CD. The U.S. Copyright Office website

(www.copyright.govhttp://www.copyright.gov/help/faq/faq-protect.html#ide)/states it this way:

"Copyright does not protect ideas, concepts, systems, or methods of doing something. You may express your ideas in writing or drawings and claim copyright in your description, but be aware that copyright will not protect the idea itself as revealed in your written or artistic work."

Many times I have had great ideas in my head (i.e. inspiration). However, I did not do anything (i.e. perspiration) to bring these inventions to reality (i.e. manifestation). And then the unthinkable happened. Someone else showed up with "my idea!" Then, I thought to myself, "Ah, the nerve of them. Someone call the police! I've been robbed! That was my idea!" I am sure that this has never happened to you. Or has it? Hmmmnnn?

The truth be told, I had not been robbed. I had been lazy. I had not performed the work necessary in order to bring my dreams to fruition. On the contrary, the person that had the same idea put in the necessary work to manifest that idea.

Thomas Edison, in my viewpoint, had a very profound work ethic. He has penned some memorable and valuable quotes regarding work and perspiration. Let us examine a few of these.

1. "There is time for everything."

The number 1,440 is truly remarkable! Wouldn't you agree? You and I see it every day. It is the number of minutes in a 24-hour day. 24 x 60 minutes = 1,440 minutes. What is even more remarkable is that we all get the same amount everyday. That's right, the successful and the unsuccessful person alike have the exact same amount of time to do great things each day.

However, it is how this time is used that makes all the difference. Oh, don't get me wrong. I used to sing the same song, too! "There isn't enough time in the day to do everything that I need to do." I once said this to the nurse attending unto my mother. And she had the nerve to tell me the exact same thing that Mr. Edison stated, "You do have enough time." Well, you know that I never told her anything personal any-more. Why, the nerve of some people (smile)!

Well, several years have passed since then. And I

have come to the conclusion that I do have enough time. A Voice spoke to my mind on one occasion and said these words, "You have just enough time to do everything that I have commanded you to do." On a more recent occasion, in rebuttal to my complaint of not having enough time, the Voice retorted, "There is a difference in what you *have* time for and what you *make* time for." And let me tell you, my brother and my sister, *finally* accepting this as truth has made all the difference in my life. Because of this acceptance, I have been able to write this book. Finally! With the same amount of time! Who would figure?

2. "*Everything comes to him that hustles while he waits.*"

It is true. There are many obstacles along the road of progress. There are realistic limitations to our dreams. These may be time, finances, space and equipment – to name a few. I have taken the "step of faith" several times. And it seemed more like taking a "step of failure." I had the "vision" but not the "provision." I remember nearly 15 years ago when I wanted to produce my first music cd. Music technology was developing, but was nothing close to what is available today. Also, I needed equipment that I could only lust at then. And in my mind, I needed to learn more chords, progressions and licks.

Well, these were all good *reasons* for not recording that cd at that time. But they were not good *excuses*. In retrospect, I could have worked at a studio in exchange for use of their instruments and equipment. I could have practiced more. Also, I could have just started with the knowledge and ability that I had at that time. The point is this: you have to keep moving and using the resources that you have at hand. Write down your vision and your plan. Share your goals and dreams with those who can and will help you. They may have another viewpoint or strategy to help you reach your goals. Don't be afraid to start out small and end up big. Above all things, start working today on your dreams and goals!

3. "*I never did anything worth doing by accident, nor did any of my inventions come by accident; they came by work.*"

One author puts it this way, "Success doesn't occur by accident: it is a planned event." Take a look at a farmer, for example. A lot of foresight and planning goes into a reaping a good harvest. They have to determine what types of crops they want to harvest. Corn? Wheat? Barley? Each seed requires a different type of soil, irrigation, and fertilization. Imagine the farmer planting seeds for a wheat harvest. And at harvest time wheat comes up. Should there be any surprise to that farmer that wheat came up? No, because it was a planned event.

Likewise, only we can determine what type of "harvest" we want in our lives. Believe it or not, many times we allow other people to determine our harvest. For example, they want a "wheat" harvest in our lives. When the reality is that we may be allergic to wheat or not even like wheat. Therefore, we must determine the type of harvest that we truly want. Then we must develop a plan to plant seeds (i.e. do work) that will bring that type of harvest. And when people ask you did you ever see yourself with this type of success, then you can respond with a resounding, "Yes!"

3. "Many of life's failures are people who did not real-ize how close they were to success when they gave up. "

My father, the late Bishop John H. Roberts was a man of great and profound wisdom. He also possessed dual "Ph.D. degrees in Suffering and Endurance." Oft times, he would encourage the members of our con-gregation to never give up any worthwhile endeavor. He was of the persuasion that "there is a high price tag for anything worthwhile in life." Bishop Roberts taught that suffering, sacrifice and discouragement were part of that price of success.

My dad used to always encourage us to take that next step towards God. He would say that, "Many of us get right to our blessings from God and then we turn around." He would then use the illustration of how he had been driving down a road trying to find a certain location. Then, feeling that he was going in the wrong direction, would make a u-turn. After fi-nally finding the location, he realized that he had been there before, but that he had turned around.

Thus, I say to you, my friend, "Walk in the direction of your heart until you reach the destination of your dreams."

4. "Our greatest weakness lies in giving up. The most certain way to succeed is always to try just one more time. "

As I look at this quote, I am reminded of the biogra-phy of Tyler Perry. He is most noted for writing and producing such hit plays as *Madea's Class Reunion* and *Diary of a Mad Black Woman*. However, everything wasn't easy from the beginning. He has experienced homelessness, hunger and despair. He candidly shares with his viewers that after many failed attempts to produce a successful play that he was going to give it all up back in 1998. He had decided to do one final production of *I Can Do Bad All by Myself*. This biography at tylerperry.com says:

"Because of having put all of his eggs in one basket, Tyler would eventually find himself homeless on one or more occasions over the following six years. Broke and at times starving, he relentlessly held on to his faith in God and continued to believe that it would all "come out all right" one day. "I know the Lord will make a way!" Perry would often exclaim.

When he did finally reach a point where he was going to give up, he reluctantly decided to do one last show. It was that one faithful decision which would change his life forever.

In the summer of 1998, what was supposed to be the "final" production of Tyler Perry's "I Know I've Been Changed" opened at the House of Blues in Atlanta and sold out eight times over. Two weeks later, the play would move to the prestigious Fox Theater and sell out 9,000 more seats for just two shows! "I Know I've Been Changed," would go on to gross several million dollars in revenue and ultimately raise the level of thinking concerning Black theater productions. Critics and audiences alike would eventually abandon the insulting title of "Chitlin Circuit", when referring to Black theater, bestowing upon it instead the respectable title of "Urban Theater."

Wow! What an accomplishment. All because he decided to give it "one more try."

Are you, my friend, like Mr. Perry, flirting with the idea of giving up you dream? Well, if you are, then I encourage you to give it one more try, and another, and another, until you reach you goal.

Don't give up! (smile)

CHAPTER 11
Hope

"Hope, in the smallest quantity,
can have the greatest effect."

If mortals die, can they live again? This thought
would give me hope, and through my struggle I
would eagerly wait for release.

-Job 14:14

There is a very inspiring story about a sick schoolboy
that appeared in the July 1991 edition of *Bits & Pieces*.
It reads:

"The school system in a large city had a program
to help children keep up with their school work
during stays in the city's hospitals. One day, a

teacher who was assigned to the program received a routine call asking her to visit a particular child. She took the child's name and room number and talked briefly with the child's regular class teacher. "We're studying nouns and adverbs in his class now," the regular teacher said, "and I'd be grateful if you could help him understand them so he doesn't fall too far behind."

The hospital program teacher went to see the boy that afternoon. No one had mentioned to her that the boy had been badly burned and was in great pain. Upset at the sight of the boy, she stammered as she told him, "I've been sent by your school to help you with nouns and adverbs." When she left she felt she hadn't accomplished much.

But the next day, a nurse asked her, "What did you do to that boy?" The teacher felt she must have done something wrong and began to apologize. "No, no," said the nurse. "You don't know what I mean. We've been worried about that little boy, but ever since yesterday, his whole attitude has changed. He's fighting back, responding to treatment. It's as though he's decided to live."

Two weeks later the boy explained that he had completely given up hope until the teacher arrived. Everything changed when he came to a simple realization. He expressed it this way: "They wouldn't send a teacher to work on nouns and adverbs with a dying boy, would they?"

Yes, hope is very powerful indeed! Its effects are far-reaching. And , amazingly enough, only a small amount is needed to accomplish great things. This chapter will discuss the following: 1) The Purpose of Hope; 2) The Power of Hope; and 3) The Provision of Hope.

1. The Purpose of Hope

What is the purpose of hope? Wow, what a tough question. However, an attempt will be made to provide an answer.

I think it important that we, first, establish a working definition for *hope*. *The Merriam-Webster Dictionary* defines *hope* as: "to expect with confidence." There are other variations to this definition, but I think that this one reveals the essence of hope: expectation.

Have you ever waited for your mail carrier to deliver that long-awaited check? Or have you seen a child on Christmas Eve waiting for Santa Claus to come and bring presents? Or have you waited to receive a telephone call from your significant other? These are just a couple of examples of hope. The expectation of these moments can override any negative circumstances. And this leads us to the purpose of hope.

I believe that the purpose of hope is to destroy "the dictates of doubt." Each of us are daily surrounded by negative circumstances that suggest that we won't make it. They try to convince us that we will fail. I see Doubt as an evil dictator that attempts to pronounce sorrow and grief on our lives. But this can only happen in the absence of hope. Because when Hope shows up –let me tell ya'- Doubt has to release its death-grip on our destinies and relinquish control to Hope! Again, I say, the purpose of hope is to destroy the dictates of doubt.

2. The Power of Hope

Hope can do what nothing else can do. It can bring life back into a lifeless situation. It can change an individual's conduct better than any rehabilitation plan. The "sun of hope" can dispel and repel any "shadow of fear." When nothing else can help – hope does!

It is simple: "When a person has something to look forward to in tomorrow, it can change how they live today. This principle is illustrated in a story that appeared in the May 1990 edition of *Today in the Word*:

> "A number of years ago researchers performed an experiment to see the effect hope has on those undergoing hardship. Two sets of laboratory rats were placed in separate tubs of water. The researchers left one set [of rats] in the water and found that within an hour they had all drowned. The other rats were periodically lifted out of the water and then returned. When that happened, the second set of rats swam for over 24 hours. Why? Not because they were given a rest, but because they suddenly had hope!

> Those animals somehow hoped that if they could stay afloat just a little longer, someone would reach down and rescue them. If hope holds such power for unthinking rodents, how much greater should its effect be on our lives."

Simply stated: "When hope is absent, people perish. When hope is present, people persist." This is the power of hope.

3. The Provision of Hope

Thus far, we have discussed the purpose of hope and the power of hope. Now, it is time to discuss how to acquire hope. This leads us to our final point of discussion for this chapter: the provision of hope.

Remember our principle regarding hope: "Hope, in the smallest quantity, can have the greatest effect." The point that I wish to emphasize here is that hope doesn't have to be big to do a big work. It is just like super glue. Unbelievably, all you need is one tiny drop in order to make things stick. Likewise, we only need "one tiny drop of hope" to make us "stick " to living and not to giving up.

That said, I have found out that hope usually comes through other people. I am a Christian minister and serve as a Bishop in the Church of Jesus Christ. And I believe that all hope ultimately comes from God alone. However, I also believe and teach that God works through people: one day at a time and one life at time. And this belief that I have isn't built on some "pie-in-the-sky" theology or philosophy. It is built on facts and results in my life over the years. Every time hope has shown up in my life it has shown up through a person, by a person or because of a person. And check this out; it was always the person that I would have never thought to bring hope to my doorstep!

I am reminded of one occasion when I was late with my car payment. At the time, I was serving as a pastor of a small congregation. And I was trying to make ends meet with the honorarium that I received each week. Well, my attempts were no good. I was late with the car payment. Then, one Sunday morning, while delivering the message, I sensed the urgency and prompting from the Spirit to tell the congregation of my situation. I outright refused. Because, in my mind, these people, like myself, didn't have it. Also, I did not want to be a burden to them. And most of all, my pride wouldn't dare let me tell them of my problem. Eventually, I obeyed what I believed to be the Spirit of God, and told the congregation of my need. I finished out the message. We dismissed. And everyone went home, with not one person replying to appeal. That was Sunday. On Monday morning someone was ringing my doorbell hysterically. I went to answer the door as fast as I could. At the door was my cousin whom I hadn't seen in years. He came in and said, "My mother called me last night and told me to get over here right away and give you the money for your car payment." He pulled the money out of his wallet, put it in my hand and left! Now, for you to fully understand the miracle of this story, you have to know about his mother (my aunt). She was living in a senior citizen home for the mentally handicapped. While in attendance at our worship services, she would be so heavily sedated by her prescription medication that she would 'appear' asleep during the service. However, this supposedly, mentally handicapped, overly medicated senior citizen had been dubbed by God to be the "Ambassador of Hope" in my life, at that time. Remember what I said before, "Every time hope has shown up in my life it has shown up *through* a person, *by* a person or *because* of a person." My aunt did not bring me the money (i.e. hope) but she caused it to be brought to me by a person. I believe to this day that God orchestrated this entire miracle.

But He did it through people. He could have let it appear out of thin air or sent it by an angel. But he didn't. Because, on the norm, God works through ordinary people.

Therefore, I encourage you to reach out to God in your own way. Believe me, He's always listening and He is always there. And furthermore, He already knows about your situation. Just give Him a chance. If you want, you can ask Him, "Please, God! Help me, like you did my brother, Dr. Roberts. Amen" Then expect with confidence to receive what you need! It can come with all the 'bells and whistles.' But it has been my experience and it is my recommendation that look for hope to come through the most unlikely of sources: average people like you and like me!

CHAPTER 12
Giving

"Pay your tithe in *percentage*; Give your offering in *public*; and Do your alms in *private*."

"Take care! Don't do your good deeds publicly, to be admired, because then you will lose the reward from your Father in heaven. When you give a gift to someone in need, don't shout about it as the hypocrites do--blowing trumpets in the synagogues and streets to call attention to their acts of charity! I assure you, they have received all the reward they will ever get. But when you give to someone, don't tell your left hand what your right hand is doing. Give your gifts in secret, and your Father, who knows all secrets, will reward you."

-Matthew 6:1-4

An insightful story about almsgiving appeared in the *Chaplain Magazine*. It reads:

"Charles Spurgeon and his wife would sell, but refused to give away the eggs their chickens laid. Even close relatives were told, "You may have them if you pay for them." As a result some people labeled the Spurgeons greedy and grasping.

They accepted the criticisms without defending themselves, and only after Mrs. Spurgeon died was the full story revealed. All the profits from the sale of eggs went to support two elderly widows. Because the Spurgeons were unwilling to let their left hand know what the right hand was doing (Matthew 6:3), they endured the attacks in silence."

I am reminded of an instance when my family was in need of alms. That is, *charity*. It was Thanksgiving Weekend 2004. A wind storm caused a tree to fall on the electrical power line running to our house. This, in turn, caused a severe electrical fire in our basement. After the fire department came and put things under control, we had to temporarily move into a hotel because we didn't have any electricity in the house. Soon, our funds were depleting and we reluctantly had to seek assistance from some charitable organizations. The American Red Cross was able to provide us with some assistance until we could get back on our feet. What was very important to us was the privacy of the transaction. The ARC didn't broadcast to everyone that they were helping us. Nor did they publicize to anyone how much assistance they were providing us. This was crucial to our dignity and our sanity at that time.

Thus, it is easy for me to begin to understand why almsgiving or charity should be a private endeavor. No one should know what is going on but the parties involved.

Look at the two widows in the illustration. I am certain that they appreciated the great lengths and sacrifice that the Spurgeons went through to keep the matter private.

On the other hand, giving an offering is totally different. It is a public event. It is a freewill testament to the bounty that a person has been blessed with.

Dr. Ed Kruse has provided some very insightful information on these subjects in his work entitled *First Mile, Second Mile and Third Mile Giving*. It provides a detailed and concise look at the three forms of giving in the ecclesiastical community.

According to Dr. Kruse, there are three kinds of financial giving in the Bible. They are: 1) Tithing; 2) Offering; and 3) Alms. He calls each of these, respectively, 1) First Mile Giving; 2) Second Mile Giving; and 3) Third Mile Giving.

Let us examine each of these in closer detail.

A. First Mile Giving: Tithing

According to Dr. Kruse, the biblical word for 'first mile giving' is *tithing*. Tithes are unrestricted and undesignated gifts to God for carrying out God's mission. This refers to the first 10% of our income. Interestingly enough, he also points out that there are instances in the Bible when the people gave a *second* and *third* tithe, also! Dr. Greogory S. Neal provides information on this topic in his work *The Second Tithe*. Dr. Neal writes:

> "The Second Tithe, as outlined in Deuteronomy chapter 14 [verses 22-23] [and Deuteronomy 26:12], was a tithe on the remaining nine-tenths of one's income which was to be set aside and used by one's family to enable the necessary observation of, and participation in, the religious festivals and feasts of the Hebrew people. These religious holidays often required the family to travel to Jerusalem and participate in the temple's sacrificial rites; the second tithe was intended to fund these pilgrimages, provide food and lodging while in Jerusalem, as well as the actual costs of the religious rites (i.e., the animals to be sacrificed). These expenses were understood to not be included within the first tithe, but rather were covered by the second tithe – a second 10% which was deducted from the nine-tenths of one's income left-over after the first tithe."

Dr. Kruse goes on to explain that another word for this type of giving is *proportionate*. That means that the tithe is the first 10% of your earnings. And it may be larger or it may be smaller than the next person's. But it should only be compared to your earnings, not someone else's. Dr. Kruse states it this way:

> "The Biblical word for first mile giving is ***"tithing."*** Tithes are unrestricted and undesignated gifts to God for carrying out God's mission. The word *tithe* denotes *ten percent*, although in the Old Testa-

ment there were several occasions on which God's people gave a second tithe and a third tithe of their crops. Another word that fits is "proportionate," "as God has prospered us" (1 Corinthians 16 and 2 Corinthians 9).

Our first mile giving is the first portion of our paycheck, rather than "leftovers" after we take care of our wants. Think of your tithe as the percent of your income that you put into your envelope to put in the offering plate. It is not relevant what the amount of dollars it may be, or whether you give more or less than I do. Your giving is based on how you are growing in comparison to your past giving. It is proportionate to how God has blessed you and continues to bless you. There is ample reference to tithing in the Old Testament. Genesis 14, Leviticus 27, Numbers 18, Deuteronomy 12, 14, and 26, 2 Chronicles 31, Nehemiah 10, 12:44, and 13, Amos 4 and Malachi 3:8 allspeak of tithes. New Testament tithing is in Matthew 23, Luke 11, 18, Romans 11:16, 1 Corinthians 16:2 and Hebrews 7. First mile giving includes growing in discipleship. First mile giving remains the fulcrum around which all other giving turns. Second mile giving presumes the joyful experience of first mile giving in one's life."

Tithing is the prerequisite for all giving. A person must first pay their tithe before they can give an offering. Which leads us to our next point: *Second Mile Giving*.

B. Second Mile Giving: Offerings

Dr. Kruse equates *Second Mile* giving with the biblical term *offerings*. As previously mentioned, offerings are any gifts in addition to the tithe. These gifts are free-will and unlimited. The giver pre-determines in their heart the amount that they want to give (see II Corinthians 9:6,7). On this subject Dr. Kruse states:

"The Biblical word for second mile giving is **"offerings."** Offerings are designated gifts. They are also gifts that are in addition to the tithe. Psalms 96:8, Hebrews 13:15 and Matthew 23:23 speak of offerings. Second mile gifts are directed to a specific cause or destination. We feel fulfilled when we see a specific way that our giving makes a difference in people's lives. This is an advantage for second mile giving. Examples of 2nd mile giving include the ELCA World Hunger Appeal, church organizations, building funds and any restricted funds. Second mile giving is over and above first mile giving. It is going the second mile. Second mile giving offers a valuable source for developing sustainable funding for ministry and mission in the church. In the Old Testament many "offerings" are mentioned, all designated for a particular purpose. There are "wave" offerings, "sin" offerings, "heave" offerings, to name a few (Exodus 25, 30, 35, 36 and 38; Numbers 5, 8, 31 and 2 Chronicles 31). Offerings are distinguished as in addition to tithes in 2 Chronicles 31:12, Nehemiah 13:5, Hosea 8:13 and Malachi 3:8. The New Testament speaks of offerings in Luke 21, Acts 21, 24, Ephesians 5 and Hebrews 10. Jesus distinguishes between tithes and offerings in Matthew 23:23."

Offerings are given publicly. This can be seen in the Old Testament references to giving offerings. Individuals would bring their offerings to the priests at the gate of the Tabernacle. It was hardly a private event. Likewise, we should give our offerings publicly. The motive here isn't to be seen and praised by men, but to publicly testify of God's goodness in our lives. I once heard Bishop William T. Cahoon of the Church of God In Christ put it this way, "We don't give to be seen, but it is nice to be seen giving." I couldn't agree more.

C. Third Mile Giving: Alms

Third Mile Giving is equated by Dr. Kruse with the biblical term *alms*. He identifies this as *situational giving* to persons less fortunate than ourselves. He writes:

"The Biblical word for third mile giving is **"alms."** Alms are situational gifts that are born out of a heartfelt desire to help someone less fortunate. It is above and beyond both first and second mile giving. The New Testament speaks of alms in Matthew 6:1-4, Luke 11:41, 12:33, Acts 3:2-31 and 24:17. It is usually a spontaneous giving. It often involves an encounter with a person who has little or nothing. When we give alms, it may come from an encounter that generates compassion. Alms are given exclusively to the less fortunate, such as the homeless, the hungry the thirsty. I think of them as the "inasmuch" people of whom Jesus says, "Inasmuch as you have done it (or not done it) unto one of the least of these my sisters and brothers, you have done it (or not done it) unto me" (Matthew 25). Street appeals come to mind. I notice a man standing on the corner with a sign, "Will Work for Food," and I know I could be in his place. I have never lost a day of eating, but I know that I did not have anything to do with the family and culture into which I was born, and maybe he didn't either. Sometimes I, like the priest and the Levite, am in too big of a hurry to give the man some money, though I can't imagine what in his mind could justify me being in that big a hurry. Beggars give me an opportunity for 3rd mile giving, however I come into contact with them. Third mile giving includes any unrestricted donations we give to less fortunate persons, whether we respond to a media announcement or to an appeal in our congregation at worship. It includes all undesignated giving through the United Way that is not included in 2nd mile giving."

So, doing alms or charity is giving to those less fortunate than ourselves. I think it important to mention here that *alms are to be done privately*. Jesus states this in Matthew 6:1-4. When it is done secretly, He says that God sees the action and rewards the giver. I can't tell you how many times I have heard people publicize and broadcast how they had helped another person in need. This is not true charity. I am a witness, true charity is just like medicine: it not only meets the financial and physical needs of a person, but it also helps to restore their dignity and character.

I know that we live in a day of charlatans, schemers and con artists. And this could turn anyone off towards doing charity. But I wish to remind you of a promise and blessing attached to giving to the poor. They are found in Psalm 41:1-3. It says:

1. Blessed is he that considereth the poor: the LORD will deliver him in time of trouble.
2. The LORD will preserve him, and keep him alive; and he shall be blessed upon the earth: and thou wilt not deliver him unto the will of his enemies.
3. The LORD will strengthen him upon the bed of languishing: thou wilt make all his bed in his sickness

Therefore, according to this passage, the person that gives to the poor will receive the following from God:

1. deliverance from trouble (verse 1)
2. preservation and long life; (verse 2)
3. blessed while on earth (verse 2)
4. deliverance from enemies (verse 2)
5. recovery from sickness (verse 3)

Not a bad deal, huh? We get all of this when we help the poor! It sounds like a win-win situation to me.

I wish to close this chapter with a poignant excerpt from the July 1990 edition of *Today in the Word*:

"Captain Levy, a believer from Philadelphia, was once asked how he could give so much to the Lord's work and still possess great wealth. The Captain replied, "Oh, as I shovel it out, He shovels it in, and the Lord has a bigger shovel.""

CHAPTER 13
Preparation

"You don't have to be scared, if you are prepared."

"The ants are not a strong folk, but
they prepare their food in the summer."
-Prov. 30:25

I remember an insightful illustration that my Dad used to share. Once upon a time, there was a hog that lived near a forest. And this particular hog loved to eat the acorns that fell from a particular oak tree. Everyday, the hog would eat these acorns until he was stuffed. Well, on one particular day, the hog went to his beloved tree expecting to gorge on acorns. And to his surprise and ultimate dismay, there wasn't a single acorn on the ground to eat!

The action of this hog is representative of some of us humans. That is, we live only here in the present and don't make any plans to prepare for the future. If the hog in our story had taken some time to think about his future, he probably would not have run out of food.

However, the lifestyle of this hog is in total contrast to that of the ant. The ant has been admired down through the ages by scientists and sages for its wisdom. The ant makes plans during its time of plenty for its time of necessity. This chapter shall briefly examine three (3) characteristics of the ant. These characteristics are it's: 1) Feebleness; 2) Foresight; and 3) Focus.

A. Feebleness

"The ants are not strong folk." These are the words of the author and wise man, Agur (Proverbs 30:25). It was his observation that the ants were not strong. In comparison to much larger animals, like the mighty lion and the mammoth elephant, the ant is truly feeble and week. Amazingly enough, although it is small, the ant is able to lift 10-50 times its own weight! Even though the ant is small, it thinks and it acts big. It performs feats disproportionately greater than its size. The ant doesn't allow its small size to become a handicap or excuse for not doing amazing and great things!

Wow! Imagine if we humans had that type of strength. That means that a person weighing 200 pounds would be able to lift upwards of 10,000 pounds! Ants are small and weak by comparison to larger animals. Likewise, humans can view or be viewed as 'small or weak." This usually happens when one human is compared and/or contrasted with another human. Often, in determining a person's worth, we usually start with their bank account. Family name, property owned, investment portfolio are some other popular criteria used to assess a person's "size" and worth. Thus, it is relatively easy to feel small and useless if you have little or none of these things.

However, lets remember the ant. It doesn't allows its size to determine its worth and ability. It starts with what it has and works from there. Also, as we shall soon see, ants work faithfully in a hierarchy with other ants. This attributes to the increase and multiplication of their strength. It has been stated before, "In unity there is strength."

And although the ant is small, it is not discouraged in making plans for its future. Likewise, although a person may have small or limited resources, they should still be motivated by the ant to make provision for their future.

This leads us to a second characteristic: foresight.

B. Foresight

At the beginning of this chapter, it was noted that the ant begins preparation for the winter in the summer. While other creatures are feasting on the spring harvest and taking it easy in the summer climate, the ant is making preparation for the winter. The Creator has given it an instinct to know what the future holds –and what it doesn't – so that it can make proper provisions to survive the winter. It knows that the food will not be as plentiful and available in the winter months as it is in the spring and summer. The ant is able to reside in the present and look into the future simultaneously. It can see today what it will need for tomorrow. The ant uses the present to make provision for the future. This is called *foresight*. It enables us to look beyond the things that we can see to the things we cannot yet see.

Like the ant, a person can greatly benefit from foresight and preparation. It is easy to become complacent and dependent upon our present employment, health and social status, to name a few. But, as many may already know, life is very dynamic. It is always changing. What is available to us today is gone tomorrow. What is certain and sure in the present becomes uncertain and unsure in the future. The reality is that companies close, our health deteriorates and that we and our loved ones eventually die. Since we know that these distasteful 'winters' are scheduled on the 'calendars of our lives,' it wise that we take a valuable lesson from the ant: *prepare for your winter during your summer.*

Foresight is the first tool in preparing for the 'winters of our lives.' It enables us to look past the things that we can see and to look into the things that we can't see. The 'summers' of our lives are the times when we have opportunity. Opportunity comes in many forms. For example, it comes in the form of youth, good health, education and gainful employment. It also comes in the form of marriage, children, family and very importantly – time. The moments that we have one, some or all of these things are the 'summers' of our lives. They should be cherished, appreciated and enjoyed. However, we must remember the rule: the summers of our lives will eventually have to give way to the winters of our lives. This is another description of *foresight:* seeing from the present what the near or distant future holds.

Preparation is the second tool in planning for the 'winters of our lives.' Foresight without preparation is worthless. It is just like the man in the story of the burning building. My Dad said that there was a man in a building that was on fire. Another tenant, upon exiting the building in haste, shouted to this man, "Hey, Mister. The building is on fire! You better get out of here!" Our subject replied, "I know." However, he never moved out of his spot and as a result, lost his life in the fire. The moral of the story is that our foresight (i.e. knowing what is going to happen) must be coupled with action (i.e. making things happen). Seeing what is coming in the future of our lives and making no preparation for it is equivalent to the hog eating the acorns without ever looking up. Proverbs 22:3 says it this way:

"A prudent person foresees the **danger** ahead and takes precautions; the simpleton goes blindly on and suffers the consequences."

Thus, developing and adhering to a preparation plan during the 'summers of our lives' will grant us provision during the 'winters of our lives.' This leads us to our third and final characteristic of the ant: focus.

C. Focus

The world that we live in is full of distractions. There are telephone calls, last-minute meetings, e-mails, bosses, noise, family and friends – just to name a few. And unfortunately, these disturbances can become deterrents to us completing our daily goals and tasks.

Not so with the ant, though. The ant isn't easily distracted from its work. In fact, it isn't distracted at all from its work. Have you ever seen ants at work in the summer in preparation for the winter? They are busy gathering and storing up their food during the summer. They don't let anything or anyone deter them from their course of action. They don't let procrastination, excuses or anything take priority over their planning and preparation. In other words: THEY ARE FOCUSED!

Likewise, we must focus on our goal: to prepare for the winters of our lives. We cannot allow distractions to disrupt our plan. Distractions are a part of life and will not go away. So, we must commit to plans and principles that aid us in reaching our goals. We must covenant within ourselves that procrastination will not rule. That excuses will not dominate. And that our 'summers' will never be wasted.

On that note, I wish to close with an excerpt from Denis Waitley's book, *Being the Best*:

"When you stop to think about it, he says, there is no such thing as a *future* decision. You face only *present* decisions that will affect what will happen in the future. *Procrastinators* wait for just the right moment to decide. If you wait for the perfect moment, you become a security seeker who is running in place, going through the motions, and getting deeper in a rut.

If I wait for every objection to be overcome, I will attempt nothing. My personal motto is, *Stop Stewing and Start Doing*. I can't be depressed and active at the same time. I like changing the word

motivation slightly to reflect a personal commitment to take charge of today and make it the best
day I can. *Motive* plus *action* equals *motive-action.*

Everybody is looking for new ways to get motivated. Companies and corporations pay sizable
fees to consultants who try to make their personnel more productive and fire up their salespeople.
A motivated person thinks, *I'm going to try it.* But
motivation must turn into motive-action, or nothing
will happen."

CHAPTER 14
Intimacy

"Intimacy has nothing to do with romance;
but it has everything to do with honesty.

"Now, although Adam and his wife were both
naked, *neither of them felt any shame."*
-Genesis 2:25

On one occasion, my father shared some insight with me about his marriage to my mother. He said, "Eddie, you know, I have been married to your mother for thirty-plus years and I am just *beginning* to understand her." In order for you to understand the impact of this statement, you would have to know my Dad. He was a man of great wisdom, experience and pride. Yet, he admitted boldly, not that he understood my Mom after 30-plus years of marriage, but that he was just *beginning* to understand her. I thought this utterly amazing for a man of his status and accomplishment to admit such a thing. It was so profound that it made me introspect and take a deep look at myself. If he was admitting that after 30-plus years of marriage that he was just beginning to know who she really was, then where did that put me as his junior by more than thirty years?! I realized then that I had a whole lot to learn about myself, about life and about women!

In contrast to my Dad, I have also heard many people claim that they *knew* their mate after only *three (3) months* of dating! I must admit, that I have been part of this group on several occasions. However, I now know that this isn't possible. In reality, it takes years and sometimes a lifetime, to know who a person truly is. This leads us to our discussion about intimacy. Men and women have different views of it. An excerpt from *"Husbands and Wives "* by *Gary Smalley and John Trent* states the following:

> *"In a Harvard study of several hundred preschoolers, researchers discovered an interesting phenomenon. As they taped the children's playground conversation, they realized that all the sounds coming from little girls' mouths were recognizable words. However, only 60 percent of the sounds coming from little boys were recognizable. The other 40 percent were yells and sound effects like "Vrrrooooom!" "Aaaaagh!" "Toot toot!" This difference persists into adulthood. Communication experts say that the average woman speaks over 25,000 words a day while the average man speaks only a little over 10,000. What does this mean in marital terms? . . . On average a wife will*

say she needs to spend _45 minutes to an hour each day_ in meaningful conversation with her husband. What does her husband sitting next to her say is enough time for meaningful conversation? _Fifteen to twenty minutes--once or twice a week!_"

As shall be discussed, communication is a major part of intimacy. But before we discuss that let's take a look at some definitions of intimacy.

A. The Basics of Intimacy

Peter K. Gerlach in his work _"Stepfamily in Formation"_ defines intimacy as:

"The dynamic process of each...[mate] trusting the safety of honestly disclosing [their] current feelings, needs, fantasies, dreams, fears, failings and limitations, general thoughts, and honest relationship feedback to [themselves] and [their] partner.

A simpler definition is ...each partner risking honest disclosure of (a) who they really are, (b) who they see their mate to really be, and (c) how satisfied they are now with their relationship."

George Graham and Hugh LaFollette define the term _intimacy_ in their work _"Honesty and Intimacy"_ as:

"An intimate encounter or exchange....in which one verbally or non-verbally privately reveals something about oneself, and does so in a sensitive, trusting way."

91

These are both excellent definitions of the term *intimacy*. However, I think that Nate Archer gives a most practical definition of *intimacy*. He writes in his work *"Intimacy"*:

"I think that nudity is actually a pretty good metaphor for intimacy! Think about it, if someone sees you naked, they are seeing THE REAL YOU! At least physically, nudity is showing off the real you, with nothing to hide. That's what intimacy is like. When you are intimate with someone, you are **_letting them see the real you_**. When you **_share your deepest thoughts and feelings with someone_**, that is intimacy. When **_you share your dreams and fears and struggles_**, that is intimacy."

So, according to Mr. Archer, intimacy occurs when we: 1) let someone see the real us; 2) share our deepest thoughts and feelings with someone; and 3) share our dreams, fears and struggles with someone

B. The Basis of Intimacy

It has been shown that the essence of intimacy is the self-disclosure of one's true self to another person. But how does this revelation take place?

Well, one way of revealing ourselves to another person is through *non-verbal* cues. Examples of this would be body language and certain behaviors (e.g. drinking, exercising, smoking, eating, reading, etc.). Simple observation of a person's daily routine can give major clues to their inner person. It has been said that you can learn more about a person by what they do than by what they say.

Another way of revealing ourselves to another person

is through *verbal communication*. In the estimation of this author, "verbal communication is the basis of intimacy." It is primarily through speech that we communicate with our partners. This can occur in a myriad of ways: telephone, e-mail, voice-mail and of course, face-to-face.

However, according to the Harvard Study at the beginning of this study, men and women place different values on verbal communication. This leads to the next sub-topic: *The Biology of Intimacy.*

C. The Biology of Intimacy

According to the Harvard Study that appears in *"Husbands and Wives "* by Gary Smalley and John Trent:

> *On average a wife will say she needs to spend <u>45 minutes to an hour each day</u> in meaningful conversation with her husband. [While] her husband sitting next to her [says] enough time for meaningful conversation [is] <u>Fifteen to twenty minutes-- once or twice a week!"</u>*

So lets do the math. According to this study, the average wife believes that **420 minutes maximum** (60 minutes x 7 days) are needed for meaningful conversation per week. Whereas, the average husband estimates that **40 minutes maximum** (20 minutes x 2 days) per week are needed for meaningful conversation. Look at the difference in these numbers: **420 minutes vs. 40 minutes**! This is quite a contrast. And this is also an excellent example of how men and women place different values of different things.

And to add this horror, one source alleges that even this abridged communication actually diminishes between marriage partners over time. The following data appeared in the *"Daily Mirror (London)"* :

> *"Married couples have nothing more to say to each other after 8 years, according to a study. Professor Hans Jurgens asked 5000 German husbands and wives how often they talked to each other. After 2 years of marriage, most of them managed two or three minutes of chat over breakfast, more than 20 minutes over the evening meal and a few more minutes in bed. By the sixth year, that was down to 10 minutes a day. A state of "almost total speechlessness" was reached by the eighth year of marriage."*

One can't help but to wonder, "Why do men and women place such different values on communication – and other things too. Well, it might have something to do with biology: the way we are made up. It is obvious that there are many physical differences between men and women. However, there are also physiological (i.e. how we act and function) differences between men and women. Peter K. Gerlach offers an excellent explanation for these differences in his work *"Stepfamily in Formation."* He states:

> *"Anne Moir and David Jessel's well researched book "Brain Sex - the Real Difference Between Men and Women" offers a clear explanation for why our gender differences exist and persist. It clearly answer's Henry Higgins' musical plaint "Why Can't a Woman Be More Like a Man?" Our*

brain structures, glands, and hormones (often) implacably prevent it, seasoned well by ancestral and social imprinting. This wired-in gender-difference in priorities (need intensities) guarantees conflict and tension, making your relationships endlessly "interesting."

Thus, the differences between men and women can be attributed to their genetic and physiological make-up. Oftentimes, these differences can negatively affect how men and women communicate. This leads to the next point: *The Barriers to Intimacy*.

D. The Barriers to Intimacy

One of the best-known stories of the Bible is that of Adam and Eve. According to the scriptures, God created both of them and placed them in the Garden of Eden to live. What sticks out most to many readers is the fact that Adam and Eve were stark naked! There were completely nude!

But what is more important than Adam and Eve being nude was the fact that they were not *ashamed*. That's right, they were not ashamed of being totally naked in front of each other. Genesis 2:25 states:

> *"Now, although Adam and his wife were both **naked**, neither of them felt any shame."*

And this verse identifies one of the most prevalent barriers to intimacy: shame

1. Shame

Many persons are ashamed of their background, past mistakes, inadequacies and faults. So, it is easy to understand why a person would rather cover up these things than expose them to their partner. Many mates believe that they will feel shame if they were to reveal any negative information about themselves to their mate.

Think about it, when we meet someone special we want to impress them. We want them to see us at our best. This is why it is natural for us to conceal rather than reveal information about ourselves.

2. Hurt

Before a person can be honest and open to another person, they must first be open and honest with themselves. I have heard it said that, "Honesty is being truthful with others. Whereas, integrity is being truthful with yourself."

According to a study, individuals of abusive childhoods experience difficulty in being honest with themselves. This dilemma persists into their adulthood. Peter K. Gerlack writes in "*Stepfamilies in Formation*":

> "True (vs. pretended, intellectual, or pseudo) intimacy between partners requires each to first be intimate with themselves - i.e. *self-aware*. Wounded survivors of low-nurturance childhoods are often used to repressing and denying these core personal factors, which cripples their ability to be empathetic and honest with themselves and each other."

Thus, many persons have difficulty with being intimate, not because they are dishonest by nature, but because they have been hurt in the past.

3. Trust

As the relationship bond grows between partners, so does trust. Trust must be earned, respected and cherished. Although, some people share their innermost secrets and desires with complete strangers, it is advisable to be intimate with trusted mates. These individuals have earned the trust of their mate.

It is difficult to 'open up' to a person that you don't trust. Simply, because you don't know what the person is going to do with the information that you share. Will they hate you for it? Will they tell the whole world? Or will they think less of you?

4. Privacy

The lack of privacy is a barrier to intimacy. Imagine sharing your deepest feelings, dreams and secrets with your mate while their entire family is listening. I don't know about you, but I wouldn't share my most cherished thoughts in a setting like that. It is important to secure an area that is devoid of distractions and interruptions. It could be by a quiet lakeside or along a sandy beach. It could be a picnic in the park or in hotel suite for two. Environments like these foster and breed intimacy. They tell the mate that, "You are important to me! You are important enough to me to get away from everybody and everything so that I can truly hear what you have to say!"

5. Loss

I believe that the ultimate barrier to intimacy is the fear of losing one's partner. Many of us believe that if we tell or show our mates who we really are, that our mates will lose respect for us and leave us. While these feelings may be true, we must remember that real relationships are built on: true love; true forgiveness; and true understanding.

If a person is willing to leave us after we have told them something precious and revealing about ourselves, then we need to ask ourselves a question: "Is this person right for me?" We all have a story to tell - and much of it isn't pretty. So, may I suggest and recommend that we be appreciative and merciful when our mates choose to be intimate with us.

E. The Benefit of Intimacy

There is one collective benefit of intimacy. According to George Graham and Hugh LaFollette in their work *"Honesty and Intimacy"* :

> "[Intimacy] enables [one partner] to understand the [the other's] behavior, to understand why one acts like one does."

What a marvelous thing! Imagine totally understanding why your mate acts the way that they do. It doesn't mean that you will necessarily like it or approve of it. But you will understand it.

Intimacy helps men and women understand more about each other. And it promises to make all of our lives the better!

CHAPTER 15
Submission

"Submission is the natural response to Love."

"Wives, submit to your husbands as to the Lord."

"Husbands, love your wives, just as Christ loved the
church and gave himself up for her."
-Ephesians 5:22, 26

I miss my Dad a lot. He was my Bishop, my pastor and
my best friend. We spent many quiet moments together. During these times he would teach me about
life through his experiences. I chuckle to myself now
as I remember him trying to teach and preach from
this text. This verse was always sure to stir hot debate
and heated emotions!

I have been honored to perform many weddings. And it is my practice to always provide pre-marital counseling before performing any matrimonial ceremonies. Many times, I have been pulled aside by the bride after the wedding rehearsal and asked what I call, "*The Question.*" "*The Question*" is, "Are you going to take out those words during the reading of the vows?" And pretending not to know, I would ask, "What words are you referring to?" And the bride-to-be would reply, "You know, those words, 'Do you promise to...obey?" And I always answer that question with a question, "Why would you be willing to marry a man that you wouldn't be willing to obey?"

This chapter will address the following topics: 1) The Definition of Submission; 2) The Prerequisite of Submission; and 3) The Requirement of Submission.

1. The Definition of Submission

Stephen B. Beck has provided a very enlightening illustration regarding *submission*. He writes:

> "Driving down a country road, I came to a very narrow bridge. In front of the bridge, a sign was posted: "YIELD." Seeing no oncoming cars, I continued across the bridge and to my destination. On my way back, I came to the same one-lane bridge, now from the other direction. To my surprise, I saw another YIELD sign posted. Curious, I thought, "I'm sure there was one posted on the other side." When I reached the other side of the bridge I looked back. Sure enough, yield signs had been placed at both ends of the bridge. Drivers from both directions were requested to give right

of way. It was a reasonable and gracious way of preventing a head-on collision. When the Bible commands Christians to "be subject to one another" (Ephesians 5:21) it is simply a reasonable and gracious command to let the other have the right of way and avoid interpersonal head-on collisions."

So, according to Mr. Beck, *submission* is: "a reasonable and gracious command to let the other [person] have the 'right of way' and avoid interpersonal head-on collisions."

The *Merriam-Webster Dictionary* defines *submission* as:

"1 a : to yield oneself to the authority or will of another **: SURRENDER b :** to permit oneself to be subjected to something <had to *submit* to surgery>

2 : to defer to or consent to abide by the opinion or authority of another"

Pamela Spurling offers the following meaning of *submission* in her article entitled *"Submission...Again."* She writes:

"But what is submission, really? Is it doing what I think is right in marriage? Is it blind obedience to every whim, request and desire my husband may have? Is submission slavery? Is it drudgery?

No... it's love.
Submission is love.

Submission is the loving desire to demonstrate the Love of God to the man He has chosen as the protector and provider.

Submission is the decision to live out what the Word of God says.

Submission is obedience.

Submission is obedience to the Word of the LORD."

And this leads back to the principle of this chapter: "*Submission is the natural response to Love.*" In other words, where there is no love, there is no submission. This leads to the second point: *The Prerequisite of Submission.*

2. The Prerequisite of Submission

In chapter 5 of this book the following definition is given for love:

"Love is not a feeling: it is a <u>covenant</u> entered into by <u>choice</u>, solely <u>committed</u> to the <u>construction</u> of a person, place or thing."

And according to Ephesians 5:22, the husband is commanded and required to love his wife. That is, according to our definition, he voluntarily enters the **covenant** of marriage by making a **choice** to **commit** to the **construction** of the life of his wife.

In the opinion of this author, no man can be a lover of his wife until he is a lover of Jesus, the Christ. The husband is given two examples by which he can gauge his love for his wife (Eph. 5:25,28,29). First, he is given the example of Jesus Christ. The husband is instructed to love his wife exactly the way Jesus loved his wife (i.e. the Church). Jesus left His paradise for her. He gave up His divine attributes for her. He endured persecution for her. He died for her. He got up (i.e. resurrected) for her. He provided for her. He is preparing a place for her. And He is coming back for her! Likewise, the husband, if he truly loves his wife, must do the same things for her that Christ did for his Wife (i.e. the Church)! Secondly, the husband is given the example of his own self. He is told to take care of (i.e. construct) his wife as he does his own body. Under normal circumstances, no man will maim, maul or destroy his own body. No, he will nurture it, pamper it, provide for it, dress it, feed it, and preserve it. Likewise, the husband is instructed to provide all of the same things for his wife!

Isaiah 9:6a foretells of Jesus Christ *loving* His bride. It states:

> "For unto us a child is born, unto us a son is given: and the government shall be upon his shoulder."

The symbolism of this verse is beautifully revealed in the weddings of the Eastern countries. In his book *"World's Bible Handbook"* Robert Boyd writes:

> "A wedding ceremony is a gala occasion in the Eastern countries. Even in all of the merriment, the

bride's face must always be covered with a veil. At the proper moment when the bride and groom are joined together, the groom removes the veil from the brides face and throws if over his shoulder. This signifies the taking of all responsibility upon himself – the government of his bride and household resting upon his shoulder."

Therefore, once love is present and once it is established, then and only then can submission be expected. This leads to the final point of this chapter: *The Requirement of Submission.*

3. The Requirement of Submission

"Submission is the natural response to Love." The prerequisite to submission is love. The husband is responsible to provide "true love" for his wife and household. Once this is provided, it is the responsibility of the wife to submit to the husband.

In her work *Submission Again* Pamela Spurling writes:

> "Submission is the decision to live your life under the authority of the husband the LORD has placed over you. Submission to your husband is key to a godly marriage and the key to submission is: just do it. That was simply said and it is simple... not easy, but simple.
>
> More importantly, a woman living in submission to her husband and to the LORD, will find that in allowing the Holy Spirit to work, her heart can be renewed, and will find created from nothing a new

love for the man. The woman committed to submission to her husband out of obedience to the LORD will encounter the heart of stone transformed into a soft heart of flesh. The submissive wife can be key to that husband's walk with the LORD. Whether he knows Him present or not, her behavior has a direct bearing on his relationship with the LORD (See 1 Peter 3).

Submission in marriage will revolutionize that marriage... and the man who has a contented wife is a man who will be free to be the man God created him to be. Every minute you step forward in faith and love that man... submitting to him and respecting him, you pave the road for him to care for, love and protect you. That's not manipulation, it's just a natural byproduct of submission. If I didn't believe this, or more importantly, if the Word of God could not be trusted, then I wouldn't write this to you.

I know some of you have fiery trials in your marriage. Some of you are married to men who really have crushed your spirit and broken your heart--------I want you to know that God never fails and His love is everlasting and He that has called you will perform all He has said...He requires that you obey and trust Him. He promises in the Word that He works everything for good..... (Romans 8.28), He will not lie and He cannot fail. You would not be where you are today unless He allowed it. Ahh... what a revolutionary thought! He loves you so much that He would even allow you to undergo a trial so that He could demonstrate His power in your life.

And William J. McRae, in his work *"Preparing for Your Marriage,"* writes:

Mrs. Martha Montgomery in her series on "The Godly Woman" gives us a helpful comparison of three related terms.

When the woman was in her unfallen state God appointed her to be *subordinate* to the man (Gen. 2:18). This was a matter of rank and did not imply any inferiority. It was an honorable position. So we see, first, a *woman* is a *subordinate*.

- This is a matter of *rank*.
- It is by God's *appointment*.
- After the woman had sinned, in her fallen state, God imposed subjection on her (Gen. 3:16).
- So second, a *woman* is in *subjection*.
- This is the matter of her husband's *rule*.
- It is *imposed* by God.
- In the New Testament the wife is enjoined to come into submission (Eph. 5:22-24) to her husband.
- Third, a woman is to be submissive.
- This is a matter of *inner attitude*.
- It is to be *voluntarily assumed*.

The inner attitude is toward the subordination appointed and the subjection imposed in Genesis. In extra-biblical Greek it was primarily a military term that denoted a rank under another. Literally the verb means *to arrange or to rank under*." The word implies a rank subordinate to one who is in authority, to whom obedience and respect are due.

106

It does not imply an inferiority of person but only subordination in rank. As a person you will be no more inferior to your husband, than the citizen is to his government or Christ is to God. Yet the citizen is subordinate in rank to the governor. Christ in His humanity was subordinate to God the Father. You are to assume volitionally and voluntarily a rank or office under your husband in the administration of your home and family.

It does not justify suppression by your husband but does imply obedience to your husband. Submission does not stifle your leadership, creativity, and initiative as a wife. You may well wonder if it implies that you will make no decisions, offer no argument, participate in no discussions. Absolutely not. What a vanilla wife you would be! What kind of a helper is this? It is not only your right but also your responsibility to function as a partner in this partnership. Every Christian husband should consult his wife as his closest advisor and make decisions with her interests in view. Often responsibilities will be delegated to you requiring important decisions that must be made by you. And yet, when your husband makes decisions, you are responsible to obey. That is submission.

Some of us know wives who do obey but are not truly submissive. A third implication in our New Testament word is that of respect for your husband in his position and for his decisions. A wife who obeys without respect is not in submission. You are to "reverence" ("fear," Eph. 5:33, same word as in v. 21) your husband. The church's reverence for Christ is your pattern. You may not agree with the decision in his position as head. The mother who enforces her husband's rules or disciplines, but lets her children know she does not agree, is not respecting her husband before her children. Such lack of respect is most often seen [in] the use of the tongue. Beware!"

In closing, "*Submission is the natural response to Love.*"

CHAPTER 16
Prophecy & Purpose

"Prophecy *tells* of things to happen;
whereas, purpose *makes* things happen."

"You can make many plans, but
the LORD's purpose will prevail."
-Proverbs 19:21

I am reminded of a remarkable story told by the late Bishop John H. Sermon. He told of one occasion, during his childhood, where both his brother and himself embarked upon an awesome quest. They had discovered a natural waterspout in their yard. According to his account, this waterspout continually gushed water out of the ground with enormous pressure. And that is when they came up with a grand idea. They decided that they would plug up this natural water source. He said that they tried everything that they could to stop the flow of water. They tried rocks, dirt and even old logs. But, none of these things were successful in stopping up the waterspout. It would simply blow all of these things out of the way and keep on flowing. Then, on one day, they met with success – well, sort of, anyway. Bishop Sermon says that his brother and himself found the heaviest stones and debris that they could find. And this time, being determined not to be outdone, they filled and stuffed the waterspout with heavier rocks and miscellaneous objects. Then, to their ultimate delight, the water stopped flowing! Feeling that they had finally accomplished their goal, he said that they began to walk away. And that is when it happened! The Bishop said that as they were walking away, that they heard a sort of rumbling in the earth. He said that they turned around to see what was happening. He testified that in one magnificent display of might and awe, that the waterspout blew out all of the rocks and debris that had been used to stanch its flow!

Like that waterspout, purpose and prophecy cannot be stopped. They can only be witnessed and experienced. They are inter-dependent. That is, they rely and depend on one another. They need each other in order to exist. Oft times, unfortunately, they are misunderstood and misapplied. As a result, this chapter shall attempt to shed some new light on some old subjects: prophecy and purpose.

A. Prophecy

Different thoughts, definitions and images come to mind when we speak of prophecy: the end of the world, doomsday and Armageddon -to name a few. While these events are *prophetic*, they are not *prophecy*.

Prophecy, according to *The Merriam-Webster Dictionary*, is:

> **1 :** an inspired utterance of a <u>prophet</u>
> **2 :** the function or vocation of a <u>prophet</u>; *specifically* : the inspired declaration of divine will and purpose
> **3 :** a prediction of something to come

Another term for *prophecy* is *forecasting*. Its definition in *The Merriam-Webster Dictionary,* is:

> **1 a :** to calculate or predict (some future event or condition) usually as a result of study and analysis of available pertinent data; *especially* : to predict (weather conditions) on the basis of correlated meteorological observations **b** : to indicate as likely to occur.

However, one of the simplest and most comprehensive definitions for *prophecy* is provided by Finis J. Dake in his book *God's Plan for Man*. He writes:

> "...Prophecy is simply history written before hand

in the same literal language as history which is a record of things that have happened. If one will take all prophecy as a simple record of what is going to happen as [one] does history as a simple record of what has happened, it will be impossible to misunderstand prophecy."

Prophecy can be further sub-divided into two types: 1) *forthtelling*; and 2) *foretelling*. *Forthtelling Prophecy* predicts and speaks of events that are occurring in the present. A common example of this is type of prophecy is preaching. *Foretelling Prophecy*, on the other hand, predicts and speaks of events that will occur in the distant future. Fred Zaspel writes in *Prophets and Prophecy*:

> "The verb "prophesy" means "to speak before" (from Greek *pro*, before, and *phemi*, to speak). The gift includes both the idea of *foretelling* and *forthtelling*, predicting the future and preaching. A prophet was God's mouthpiece: he spoke for God and gave His message. Sometimes that message was regarding the future. Other times it concerned the present, even the past, or simply doctrinal truth, but it was always God's message spoken forth."

Simply, prophecy is declaration. But in order for there to be *declaration* there must be *documentation*. That is, prophecy has to get its information from a reliable, written source. And that source is: *Purpose*.

B. Purpose

In the opening illustration, the flow of the waterspout could not be stopped. It was temporarily delayed, but could not be ultimately stopped. In like manner, purpose cannot be stopped. One can cooperate with it or one can conflict with it, but one cannot stop it.

But, what does the term 'purpose' mean? *The Cambridge Advanced Learners' Dictionary* provides the following definition for *purpose*:

> **"1** [C] why you do something or why something exists:"

Another definition for *purpose* is provided by Myles Munroe in *"Releasing Your Potential*. He writes that:

> *"Purpose* is the reason why something was made. It is the ends for which the means exist."

It has been stated that, "Purpose makes things happen." But how is this so? Well, the secret lies in the illustration of the waterspout. Remember? Nothing could stop its flow: not rocks, not soil, not anything. Well, likewise, nothing can stop purpose. The reason that nothing can stop ultimate purpose is because ultimate purpose is supplied with ultimate power. It is the driving force (i.e. reason) for life. *Power*, in terms of physics, relates to the ability to produce an effect. This is the essence of purpose: to produce desired effects based on the design and desire of the Creator. As a result, human devices, natural forces, nor historical events don't affect purpose. But human invention, natural phenomena and history are *affected* by purpose. Purpose is not reactive; it is proactive.

True purpose can be likened to a moving train. It has _drive_ (i.e. the engine). It has _direction_ (i.e. the train tracks). And it has _destination_ (i.e. the ultimate goal /reason). Passengers can relate to a moving train in at least one of four ways: 1) They can get on the train; 2) They can get off the train; 3) They can miss the train; or 4) They can get run over by the train!

Likewise, people can cooperate with purpose (i.e. get on the train). And they may disagree with purpose (i.e. get off the train). Or people can even misunderstand purpose (i.e. miss the train). But, unfortunately, some people try and stop purpose. And they are like people standing in front of a speeding train: they get run over! It is written in Proverbs 19:21:

> "You can make many plans, but
> the LORD's purpose **will** prevail."

An anonymous story appears on *sermonillustrations.com*:

> "Matthew Henry went to London, met a young lady of the nobility, who was also wealthy, and they fell in love. She went to ask her father if she could marry him and he said, "He's got no background, you don't know where he's come from." She said, "Yes, I know, but I know where he's going and I want to go with him."

And just like that young lady saw the destiny of Matthew Henry and desired to go with him, we can see the destiny of Purpose and should desire to go with it. It is, therefore, my recommendation that we all "hitch a ride with purpose." I believe that this is the reason that you and I are still here. Purpose has pre-determined that our existence is complimentary to its program. And therefore, we have been spared from death and granted life –one more time! And it is a surety: the person who partners with purpose, partners with success! Life's challenges and uncertainties may seem to set us back at times. But these are only temporary situations for those of us who are on board with purpose. Just like the waterspout in our illustration, we cannot be stopped. This is simply because of the fact that purpose can not be stopped!

In summation, prophecy is the mouthpiece of purpose. Without Prophecy, Purpose is mute. I believe that before Prophecy speaks, that it leans over and gently taps the shoulder of Purpose to ask it where it has been, where it is now and where it is going. Then, once Prophecy completes its conference with Purpose, it stands upon the highest mountain peaks, along the vastest plains and in the lowest valleys of history to declare the course of Purpose.

CHAPTER 17
Leadership

"Leadership isn't forcing people to do things;
actually, it is inspiring people to do things."

"Without wise leadership, a nation falls;
with many counselors, there is safety."
                                    -Proverbs 11:14

Dr. Guy Brewer shares an inspiring story in his work *There's Gold in Them There Pews*. He writes:

"Andrew Carnegie, American industrialist, employed forty-three millionaires at the height of his success. When asked how he made millionaires, Carnegie talked about mining gold.

You develop people the same way you mine gold. To mine gold, one digs several tons of dirt to get an ounce of gold. But one does not go into the mine looking for dirt. One goes in looking for gold."

This illustration brings to mind one of the greatest leaders that I have ever known: my Dad, the late Bishop John H. Roberts. Like Mr. Carnegie, he possessed the innate ability to "see the gold" in other people. I know this to be true, because I am one of those persons. It was through him that I received my primary leadership training. I remember his words to me concerning my vocation as a Christian leader. He taught me that my job isn't to excite and entertain people. My job is to give people accurate information that will encourage them to think about and improve their lives! I never accepted my calling to Christian leadership because of what my Dad preached in public. No, I accepted my calling based on the life that he lived in private. He provided me with a higher vision of myself. He challenged me to do more with my life. And he encouraged me to be the person that not only he admired, but that others could admire also.

Simply, leadership primarily entails seeing and developing potential in others. It commences with believing in people and teaching them to believe in themselves. True Leadership inspires people to set new challenges and goals for themselves. Peter Drucker says the following regarding leadership:

"Leadership is not magnetic personality. That can just as well be a glib tongue. It is not making friends and influencing people; that is flattery. Leadership is lifting a person's *vision* to higher sights, the raising of a person's *performance* to higher standards, the building of a *personality* beyond its normal limitations."

Three words stand out here: 1) vision; 2) performance; and 3) personality. I see these as three (3) major components of leadership.

Like Andrew Carnegie saw "gold" in his workers, and like my Dad saw "gold" in others and myself, the eagle too, sees "gold" in its young. Interestingly enough, the mighty, bald eagle is a ubiquitous symbol for leadership. I believe that several parallels exist between 'eagle development' and 'leadership development.' This chapter will examine the habits of the eagle and how they relate to three (3) major components of leadership: 1) Vision; 2) Performance; and 3) Personality.

1. Vision

When the young eagling is first born, the mother eagle lines the bottom of the nest with soft, downy feathers from captured prey and even her own breast. This makes for a nice and comfortable bed for this young eagle. In addition, the adult eagles bring food daily to the eagling in the nest and literally place it in its mouth! The young eagle wants for nothing, because the parents provide it with everything – at least for a little while. After providing for the eagling for a while, the mother eagle begins to do something very strange. She begins to pluck up the soft feathers from the bottom of the nest and throw them overboard. These are the same feathers that she had previously placed down in the nest! Finally, she throws the entire nest down the side of the mountain.

There is a plausible explanation for the mother eagle's behavior. Once the eagling reaches a certain age, the mother eagle instinctively knows that it is time for her eaglet to learn how to fly! She has a "vision" of what that young eagling really is. Jacque Koivuniemi writes in *On Eagles Wings*:

> "The mother eagle watches her baby eaglets carefully; as they grow, she stirs them up a bit so they will not be contented to lie in the nest: she then flutters over them to make them want to use their wings as she does."

Both the mother eagle and the father eagle provide a prototype of what a true eagle looks like and what a true eagle acts like.

Just like the eagle, effective leaders have the ability to see (i.e. vision) leadership qualities in other leaders. They can't put them there, for that is the job of the Creator. But they can identify them, for that is the job of a leader. I remember when I was accepted into a national youth leadership development program. The first thing that they told us was that they could not make us leaders: we had to already be leaders. They could only 'mine' and develop the leadership quali- ties that we already possessed. A fellow Christian pastor, Javon Allen of the Church of God in Christ pointed out to me that you can't train a follower to be a leader; you can only train a leader to be a bet- ter leader.

A leader is a role model, a prototype of sorts. He or she must serve as the epitome of what the other leaders can and must become. The leader is a visual manifestation of a mental ideation. It is easy for the eaglet to know what it can look like and what it can do by simply looking at its parents. A good leader will enable other leaders to see a higher vision of themselves. As a personal rule, I don't follow any leader that has equal or less than what I have. This is because I believe that the life and the status of the leader is the ultimate hope of the follower. What you see is what you get. If the leader is a loser, then the follower, at best, can be a loser. If the leader is average, then the follower, at best, can be average. But, if the leader is great, then the follower, at best, can be great! To substantiate my point, let's take a look at major, corporate sponsors. When these companies want to launch a huge marketing campaign to sell their products, who do they use? Celebrities! They use celebrities. Why? Because, they want to associate their product with success and winning (hint: great leadership). Nike, for instance, doesn't use losing or mediocre athletes to endorse its products. It only uses winners!

Likewise, great leaders serve as icons of success and winning. And this image serves as the goal of the group that the leader serves. Dr. John Haggai writes in *Lead On!*:

> "Leadership is the discipline of deliberately exerting special influence within a group to move it towards goals of beneficial permanence that fulfills the group's real needs."

2. Performance

After the mother eagle destroys the nest, she scoops the eagling onto her back. She then flies high up into the sky. While airborne, the mother eagle flips over and darts out from underneath the young eagle. The young eagle begins to try and fly. The father eagle watches carefully to see if the young eagle can fly. If he sees that it cannot fly, he will swoop down at speeds up to 200 mph to catch the young eagling before it hits the ground. He then returns the young eagle to the cliff. The eaglet does not learn to fly overnight. This cycle continues until the young eagle learns to stretch out its wings and soar like the adult eagles. The following information about eagle flight training appears in "The Cupbearer Journal" by Cary Broughton:

> "Most Eaglets do not learn how to fly the first time they try; however, they continue the flight process until they have accomplished the goal of flying. Once the Eaglet learns to fly, the papa and mama Eagle [fly] in a circle in celebration…The adult Eagle has five primary feathers on each wing. This is so the Eagle can adjust his wings during long training fights to keep the Eaglet from falling to the ground while teaching him to fly. The Eaglet is always under the power of his father during training."

So, let's review the progression of the young eagle's performance. The eaglet starts out in a comfy 'penthouse' where it consumes everything and produces nothing. That is until the mother eagle (i.e. leader) realizes and sees (i.e. vision) that it is time for the young eagle to leave the nest, learn to fly and live on its own. The mother eagle destroys the nest. In co-operation with the father eagle, the mother eagle teaches the young eagle how to fly and to fend for itself.

Effective leadership, both requests and requires superior performance. As fore stated by Peter Drucker:

> "Leadership is.... the raising of a person's *performance* to higher standards."

In our illustration, the mother eagle "raises the performance standards" of the young eagle. She does this by creating conditions that make the eagling leave the nest and learn to fly. The truth is that people, on the norm, are not naturally motivated to seek out higher levels of performance. This is one of the major purposes of good leadership. George Barna writes in *How to Find Your Church*:

> "Leadership is the ability to put the plans into practice, and to accomplish the specified objectives through the skillful management of people, time, and tangible resources. A good leader is one who is able to motivate people; one who is capable of making good decisions, even under pressure or in conditions of uncertainty; one who can guide people through actions as well as words."

Good leadership will inspire individuals to lift themselves to a higher level of performance. This reminds me of an ancient Chinese proverb. It says:

> "Go to the people. Live among them, learn from them, love them. Start with what they know, build on what they love, and, as with the greatest of leaders, when our work is done, the people will say, 'we have done it ourselves."

3. Personality

Many animals have instinct to know when a storm is approaching and will retreat into hiding. But, this isn't so with the eagle. The eagle, like many other animals, knows when a storm is coming, long before it breaks. However, unlike other animals, it doesn't retreat to find cover from the storm. No, the eagle knows how to "ride out the storm" –literally. Jacque Koivuniemi writes the following in *On Eagles Wings*:

> "Did you know that an eagle knows when a storm is approaching long before it breaks? The eagle will fly to some high spot and wait for the winds to come. When the storm hits, it sets its wings so that the wind will pick it up and lift it above the storm. While the storm rages below, the eagle is soaring above it. The eagle does not escape the storm. It simply uses the storm to lift it higher. It rises on the winds that bring the storm. "

Therein, it is seen that the eagle does not run from a storm. It anticipates it by instinct (i.e. blowing winds).

It prepares for it by position (i.e. high cliff). And it endures it by convection (i.e. updraft winds).

Just like the eagle, good leadership doesn't run from a storm; it weathers it. Like the eagle, good leadership will proactively anticipate "storms" and prepare for them. Experienced leadership knows how to ride out the "trend-winds." It also instills a sense of calm and confidence in the rest of the team. Tom Landry, former head coach of the Dallas Cowboys football team said:

> "Leadership is a matter of having people look at you and gain confidence, seeing how you react [to a storm]."

The ultimate test of leadership is not how one performs when everything is going well, but how one performs when everything is going wrong. The late Reverend Dr. Martin Luther King, Jr. stated:

> "The ultimate measure of a [person] is not where [they] [stand] in moments of comfort and convenience, but where [they] [stand] at times of challenge and controversy."

As I prepare to close this chapter, I am reminded of the first time that I had to provide consolation to a bereaved family. A dear member of our congregation, Sister Shelia Ferguson, had passed away. I went to the hospital that night to perform the last rights over her body. After that, I went to her house to meet with her family and loved ones. By the time I returned home, I was a nervous wreck. I tossed and turned all night. The next morning, my father, who was my pastor at the time, counseled me. He politely, but sternly, explained to me that I couldn't allow myself to be weak at that time and fall apart. He explained that the bereaved family needed to see one thing in me: strength. He added, "If they see you falling apart, then they will fall apart, too." He was right. And with God's help, I heeded my father's advice and regained my composure and strength. As a leader, I chose to be strong in a time of weakness. And as a result, those that were weak were able to become strong!

CHAPTER 18
What God Allows

"There is a difference between what God allows
and what God approves."

*"God overlooked people's former ignorance about
these things, but now he commands everyone everywhere to turn away from idols and turn to him."*
                                                    -Acts 17:30

Many people ask the question, "If God is good, then
why does He allow bad things to happen in the
world?" One plausible explanation is this: what God
allows and what God approves of are two totally different things." Another explanation is that God is
longsuffering and patient. He is always giving a person the maximum amount of time to change their
mind and their ways (i.e. repentance). From the be-

ginning of time, God has allowed sin, only in the hopes that people would change. But he has never approved of sin. This brings to mind a story by Thomas Lindberg. He states:

> "According to a traditional Hebrew story, Abraham was sitting outside his tent one evening when he saw an old man, weary from age and journey, coming toward him. Abraham rushed out, greeted him, and then invited him into his tent. There he washed the old man's feet and gave him food and drink. The old man immediately began eating without saying any prayer or blessing. So Abraham asked him, "Don't you worship God?
>
> The old traveler replied, "I worship fire only and reverence no other god."
>
> When he heard this, Abraham became incensed, grabbed the old man by the shoulders, and threw him out his tent into the cold night air.
>
> When the old man had departed, God called to his friend Abraham and asked where the stranger was. Abraham replied, "I forced him out because he did not worship you.
>
> God answered, "I have suffered him these eighty years although he dishonors me. Could you not endure him one night?"

The manner in which God deals with people can be seen in the way that parents deal with their children. Parents normally have different levels of expectation from their children. This is usually based on at least three (3) factors: 1) age; 2) awareness; and 3) ability. Usually, a parent will tolerate behavior from their infant child that they won't dare tolerate from their teenage child. For example, if the infant child inadvertently knocks over and breaks a vase on the kitchen table, that infant isn't normally punished or disciplined for this act. On the other hand, if the teenage child knocks over the same vase, that child will normally receive some type of reprimand. Why the difference? While some may claim favoritism or preferential treatment, the reason has a lot to deal with: age, awareness and ability. Concisely stated, the infant isn't the same age as the teenage sibling and therefore, doesn't have the same level of awareness and ability. However, the parent will not accept this type of behavior from their infant child forever. As the infant child grows and matures, their level of responsibility and accountability grows also. Why? It is common to hear parents say, "Because you are older now and you know better!"

This is representative of how God deals with humans. There is a time when we, just like newborn babies, are innocent and ignorant of His commands. Knowing this, God exercises mercy and tolerates our shortcomings. He allows us to commit certain sins without much discipline. If one didn't know any better, it would seem that God was actually approving our sinful lifestyle. But, He is not. He is simply allowing it until we come into higher knowledge and understanding of Him. Like the parent, there comes a day in each of our lives when God demands that we become accountable for our actions. My Mom used to always say, "As you come to the Light, walk ye therein." She meant that there are many things about God and His ways that we don't know (i.e. ignorance). And, as a result, we unknowingly disobey and dishonor Him.

But, she explained that there comes a time in our lives when God reveals higher knowledge to each individual. And it is at this time that we should elect to comply with His commands.

"There is a difference between what God allows and what God approves." As seen in the opening illustration, the stranger had been 'endured' or tolerated by God. He did not approve of this man's lifestyle at all. However, God dealt (i.e. suffered) with this man for eighty years, even though He did not approve of his lifestyle. And, on top of that, He chided Abraham for not dealing with this abhorrent, repulsive man for at least one more night. Why? Why would God do such a thing? Why would He 'waste' so much time on a person who obviously didn't care for Him nor respect Him? There are at least three (3) reasons for God's behavior regarding this man. And these are the same reasons that He permits people to temporarily live against His laws, even though He doesn't approve of their lifestyles. These three reasons are: 1) choice; 2) chance; and 3) change.

1. Choice

A dog has to bark. A bear has to hibernate. And a fish has to swim. The reason for this is because of one word: instinct. These are all animals and they have to do these because their instinct makes them do these things.

But human beings are totally unique from the rest of nature. Humans possess a gift that no other creature in the universe possesses. And that gift is: choice. The privilege and ability of free choice is what distinguishes humans from the rest of creation. Each human being, from the infant to the centenarian, possesses free will. And, without a doubt, choice is power.

Humans have the ability to choose their own destinies. We can choose our schools, our careers and our mates. We can decide where we want to live. Humans make decisions ranging from naming their pets to selecting the benefactors of their wills. Indeed, the power of choice is a great privilege.

Also, choice determines who and what we believe in. And, it also determines who and what we don't believe in. And this is where God comes in. He can't and won't override our free will. Even though He knows what it is best for us, He cannot and will not make a choice for us. Only we can do that. Like any good parent, He will offer you advice. He will give you both sides and the consequences involved with both (Deut. 28). And then He hopes that you make the right decision.

Thus, this is why a person can know God's laws, disobey God's laws and still live for a period of time. They aren't alive because God approves of their lifestyle. Simply, God respects their right to choose their own destiny. And He will give them the largest window of opportunity possible, in which to make this decision. This leads to the second reason: Chance.

2. Chance

Each day can truly be viewed as a gift from God. Because, with each new day comes the chance to make a choice to follow God. Humans can only make these decisions while they are alive. So, each day that God allows a person to live a life that He doesn't approve of is a chance to make a choice. Many times God offers us chances to choose Him, but unfortunately, we don't take advantage of them. William Moses Tidwell illustrates this concept through a story in his book "Effective Illustrations":

"On his birthday, a very wealthy man in London called his servants together to give them some presents. He had a Bible and some twenty-dollar notes. The servants were to make a choice between the Bible and the notes.

First came the gardener, who said, "I would like to have the Bible, but my wife is very sick and I need the money. I will take the note."

The cook said, "I can't read, so the Bible would not do me any good. Give me the money."

The coachman said, "I would appreciate having the Bible, but I have some pressing obligations. I believe the money will help me more."

Finally the errand boy came for his gift. The old gentleman asked, "Son, which will you take?"

The boy replied, "I really need the money, but my mother, who has gone to heaven, used to read to me from the Bible. I will take that"

The old gentleman was very much pleased with this choice. As he handed the good Book to the boy, he said, "God bless you, my son, for your wise choice. I present this Book to you with all it contains."

All the servants were still sitting in the presence of their master. The boy slowly opened the pages of the Book. A shining twenty dollar gold piece dropped out. This, the boy picked up and handed to the donor of the Book.

"No," said the old man, "did I not give you the Book with all that it contained?" The boy continued to turn the pages, and all along through the Book he found large bank notes. When these were counted, they proved to be quite a fortune.

The other servants sat back, quite abashed in the presence of the boy whose' choice had meant more than he had known.

So it is when one chooses Christ. If we are true, it means salvation, peace and happiness in this world and a mansion in the better world through all eternity."

Therein, taking advantage of a chance to choose Christ will result in profitable alterations in one's life. This leads to the final reason: Change.

3. Change

I read sometime ago that, "The end of all teaching is a change in behavior." And that is all that God is after in our lives: change. Actually, this is the root meaning of the term 'repent.' It simply means "*to change one's mind*." It is fact, when our attitude changes, then our actions change.

There is a heart-wrenching story that illustrates the

marvelous change that comes from making the right choice. Warren Wiersbe, in his book *Wycliffe Handbook of Preaching & Preachers,* shares the following:

> "While waiting in a cemetery to conduct a funeral service, Charles Simeon walked among the graves, looking at the epitaphs. He found one that arrested him:
>
> > *When from the dust of death I rise,*
> > *To claim my mansion in the skies,*
> > *E'en then shall this be all my plea—*
> > *"Jesus hath lived and died for me."*
>
> He was so impressed with that gospel message that he looked for someone in the cemetery with whom he might share it. He saw a young woman, obviously distressed, and called her over to read the epitaph. He took her address and visited her the next day. The home was a scene of poverty and squalor. The woman's old mother was dying of asthma, and two little children, very dirty, were trying to warm themselves by a small fire. Simeon prayed with the family, visited them again, and found assistance for them. Later, the young woman told Simeon that she had been in the cemetery five hours and was contemplating suicide when he called her to read the epitaph. Because of his concern she trusted Christ and the family situation was changed. "

Thus, it can be seen why God allows us to live lives of which He doesn't approve. He is giving us a *chance* to make a *choice* that will *change* our lives forever!

CHAPTER 19
Finances

"Seek to live beneath your means,
not within them."

"The wise man saves for the future
but the foolish man spends whatever he gets."
-Proverbs 21:20

Money. It makes the world go around. Even the Bible says that, "...money is the answer for all things." There are three classes of people in regards to money. The first class consists of people who have money. The second class consists of people who don't have money. And the third class consists of people who had money, but don't have it anymore. It is a fact: everyone manages their money differently. Some manage it well and some don't. Poor money management is a major crisis in the world today. Just look at the government and consumer deficits. Poor money management can be traced back to three factors: 1) no planning; 2) overspending; and 3) over-extending. George Fooshee provides some staggering statistics in the April 1987 edition of *Homemade*. He states:

"...Since statistics show that the average American consumer has installment payments equal to 17 to 18 percent of his take-home pay, obviously large numbers of persons are overspending. An increase in bankruptcies of over 50% more each year than the previous year, would indicate that such overspending is leading many into financial disasters. And the Bible calls such spenders fools! I don't know many people who deliberately choose to be foolish. When it comes to money, the way to be wise is to be a saver. Here are four simple rules given by the late financier, J.P. Morgan, for saving money. 1. Start early. Today is the day to start your savings program. 2. Save a definite amount. 3. Save regularly and systematically. 4. Employ your savings productively."

This chapter will provide the reader with some financial tools for good money management. Please note that the author isn't a financial consultant. So, please consult with your financial advisor before using any of these tools.

Our Financial Toolkit consists of five (5) primary tools: 1) Budgeting; 2) Expenses; 3) Savings; 4) Investments; and 5) Purchasing. Let's take a look at our first tool: budgeting.

1. Budgeting

The most important step in sound financial planning is: writing down your budget. It can serve as your 'roadmap' to help you reach your financial destinations (i.e. goals). Also, it will help you foresee and avoid any 'accidents' along the way. The term 'accidents' refers to, but isn't limited to: bank overdrafts, late fees, repossessions, late payments, and bankruptcies. Your budget consists of two primary sections: 1) Income; and 2) Expenses. It is wise to tabulate all sources of income (e.g. salary, pension, benefits) for a particular month. This figure represents your total monthly income. The next step is to categorize and itemize all of your monthly expenses. One way to do this is design a table or grid with the following headings: 1) name of vendor; 2) date due; 3) amount due; 4) date paid; and 5) amount paid. Here is a **Sample Budget**.

Sample Budget: July

	Date Due	Amt. Due	Date Paid	Amt. Paid
Income				
ABC Employ-ment	07-01	$1400.00		
Part-time Job	07-05	$500.00		
Total Income		$1900.00		
Expenses: July 15th				
Tithes	07-15	$190.00	07-15	$190.00
Offering	07-15	$50.00	07-15	$50.00
Mortgage	07-15	$400.00	07-15	$400.00
Car Pay-ment	07-15	$418.00	07-15	$418.00
Car Insurance	07-15	$134.00	07-15	$134.00
Student Loan	07-15	$125.00	07-15	$125.00
Cellular Phone	07-15	$80.00	07-15	$80.00
Total Expenses		**$1427.00**		**$1427.00**
Total Savings	**07-15**	**$473.00**	**N/A**	**N/A**

"Sample Budget A"

This sample budget gives projections of the *total monthly income, the total monthly expenses* and *the total monthly savings.* It can prove very helpful in planning your finances.

2. Expenses

Regarding expenses, there are two recommendations: 1) Pay your tithe; and 2) Pay the smallest bill first.

a. Pay Your Tithe

Note that the tithe is listed as an expense. Some people don't believe in paying a tithe. And that is their right. May God be merciful to them. But for those of us who do believe in paying our tithe, it is advisable to view it as an expense. The tithe should be viewed just like the federal income tax that is deducted from our payroll checks. The government doesn't ask, nor does it wait, it simply takes its money off the top. And many times it takes too much. Once a year, the government will acknowledge that it has taken too much of your money. And it provides it in the form of an *income tax refund.*

Thus, if we can pay the government its money without any contention, surely we can pay the tithe to the '*Higher Government*' without contention.

b. Pay the Smallest Bill First

It is good business practice to pay all bills on time and in full. However, many times a person can fall short of this goal. One strategy in eliminating debt is to pay the smallest debt first.

In "Sample Budget A" the smallest expense is the $80 cellular phone bill. If it were not to possible to pay all of the bills on time, due to a myriad of reasons, a possible strategy is to pay off the cell phone bill. The next month, use the $80 that would normally have been used to pay the cellular phone bill to pay the next expense with the lowest amount due. Continue to employ this cycle until you have eliminated all of your debts.

3. Savings

I am thankful for the wisdom of father. He always stressed the importance of managing one's finances with great thriftiness and frugality. I would like to share three (3) of his most prominent teachings concerning money.

a. How much you make vs. How much you save.

My Dad always used to say, "It isn't how much money you make that counts; but its how much you save that counts." And over the years I have found this to be true –usually around tax time (smile). When you look at how much you made and how much you have left, you can feel like you have been robbed. Where did all of that money go? Without a written budget it is difficult to tell.

I remember when my budget was $50 per week. Can you believe it? Fifty dollars! And I couldn't wait until the day that I would make $500 per week. Well, eventually that day came and I was making much more than $500 per week. And I lived happily ever after, right? Wrong. The truth was that I did more with that $50 per week than I did with that $500 per week. What happened? Well, I succumbed to one of the oldest human trends: the more we make, the more we tend to spend. If I had continued to manage that $500 plus per week like I had managed that $50 per week, then my finances would have been in great shape. I have to agree with Dad, "It isn't how much you make that matters; but its how much you save that counts."

b. Save What You Won't Miss

My Dad used to always say, "Save an amount that you won't miss." His recommendation was something like $5 or $10 per week. The 'method behind his madness' was this: if you miss what you put away into savings, eventually you will go back, withdraw it and spend it. And it is usually a good reason that makes one spend their savings. It can be a mortgage payment; college tuition, medical bill and the like.

My Dad was serving in World War II when this wisdom was first shared with him. He, like many of us, thought that this amount was too small and tried to save big. And just as expected, life's emergencies consumed his meager savings. He often expressed his regret for not following that advice to save small over a long period of time. For the sake of it, let's do the math:

Fifty (50) years x $520
(52 weeks @ $10 per week) = **$26,000**

And this figure doesn't even include the interest calculated and compounded over a 50-year period! I purchased a book sometime ago and I believe that its title recommends how we should save. Its title is: "Get Rich Slow."

c. "Never Spend Your Last Penny."

My father used to love to sit and count his money. More importantly, he hated to depart from it. And he used to encourage our family and congregation to hold on to their money as longs as possible through wise management. He used to always admonish us with these words, "Never spend your last penny." My Dad didn't believe in ever being broke. Believe you me; he always had a stash somewhere –ask my Mom (big smile).

There is a lot of merit to this financial principal of never spending your last penny. Simply, because it is connected to another financial principal: money attracts money. Just by observation, over the years, I have found this to be true. Look at who wins big at the casino: usually the person that already has money. Look at whom the banks lend money to: many times it's the person that already has money. Look at whom the restaurants give 'free' dinners to: the celebrities. Many of them could buy the restaurant if they wanted. And here they are receiving free meals. Why? Because they are experiencing the benefits of the principle: money attracts money.

So, when you spend your last penny, you become broke. And from a principal-based standpoint, when you are broke, you can't attract money. So, the best advice is to "never spend your last penny."

4. Investments

a. *Give Your Offering*

The offering is any amount above and beyond the tithe. For example, if your tithe is $73.46, one penny or more above that amount is considered an offering.

The offering is totally voluntary. This means that the giver pre-determines the amount that they will give. No one has the right to force or demand a certain amount for an offering. However, they can make a request. Then, if the giver is willing, that amount can be given. It is extremely important that the giver be willing to give whatever amount that they give. Look at what the Bible says about this in 2 Corinthians 9:7a,b:

> "You must each make up your own mind as to how much you should give. Don't give reluctantly or in response to pressure. " (TLB)

When a person is willing to give a certain amount, then it is easy for that person to be happy in giving that amount. This is vital, because 2 Corinthians 9:7c adds that "God loves a cheerful giver" –not a tearful giver.

Note that giving your offering is placed under investments. Why is this? Well, according to the Bible, the more that a person gives in the offering, the more that God blesses them with. According to 2 Corinthians 9:6,8:

> "Remember this--a farmer who plants only a few seeds will get a small crop. But the one who plants generously will get a generous crop...And God will generously provide all you need. Then you will always have everything you need and plenty left over to share with others."

So, when you give an offering, you are not only investing in God's kingdom, but you are investing in your own kingdom, too!

b. Do your alms

Doing alms or *charity* is giving to those less fortunate than ourselves. I think it important to mention here that *alms are to be done privately.* Jesus states this in Matthew 6:1-4. When it is done secretly, He says that God sees the action and rewards the giver. I can't tell you how many times I have heard people publicize and broadcast how they had helped another person in need. This is not true charity. I am a witness, true charity is just like medicine: it heals not only the financial and physical needs of a person, but it also helps to restore their dignity and character.

I know that we live in a day of charlatans, schemers and con artists. And this could turn anyone off towards doing charity. But I wish to remind you of a promise and blessing attached to giving to the poor. They are found in Psalm 41:1-3. It says:

1. Blessed is he that considereth the poor: the LORD will deliver him in time of trouble.
2. The LORD will preserve him, and keep him alive; and he shall be blessed upon the earth: and thou wilt not deliver him unto the will of his enemies.
3. The LORD will strengthen him upon the bed of languishing: thou wilt make all his bed in his sickness.

Therefore, according to this passage, the person that gives to the poor will receive the following from God:

- deliverance from trouble (verse 1)

- preservation and long life; (verse 2)

- blessed while on earth (verse 2)

- deliverance from enemies (verse 2)

- recovery from sickness (verse 3)

Not a bad deal, huh? We got all of this when we help the poor! It sounds like a win-win situation to me.

c. "Don't work for money, but make your money work for you."

Dad used to always say, "Don't work for money, but make money work for you." He thought it detestable to go to jobs that we hated and to live from pay-check to paycheck.

My father was an entrepreneur and instilled that same spirit into his children. He used to tell us, "You will never get rich by working for someone else; the only way that you will ever get rich is by owning your own business!" Countless times, Dad encouraged my siblings and myself to pool our finances together and purchase real estate property. Then he told us to use the profits from that property to purchase another, and another, and another until we could all retire young!

This is what Dad meant when he said, "Don't work for your money, but make your money work for you."

5. Purchasing

a. "Everyday Can't Be Christmas!"

When I was a little boy, everyday my Dad would buy me a toy. Actually, I don't remember this, but he claims that it happened and I won't argue the point (smile). Nevertheless, I do remember the day when I began to work and earn an income. I believed then that I was entitled to anything that I could afford. After all, it was my money. I worked for it. And I could do whatever I wanted to with it. Right? Wrong! My Dad attempted to deliver me from this destructive mindset with these words, "Eddie, everyday can't be Christmas!"

What did he mean by these words? He was simply telling me that I couldn't buy everything that I desired anytime I wanted. Dad emphasized that a portion of my salary should be for normal expenses, but that the bulk should be for savings and investments. Oh, how right he was!

It is true, "everyday can't be Christmas." It is unwise to spend all of one's earnings on useless products and services. However, it is very wise to pay one debts on time and to save and invest the rest.

b. "It Isn't a Sale if You Don't Need It"

One of the popular highways in my area is Route 22. Two lanes run east and west, from New Jersey to Pennsylvania. It is a shopper's paradise. It has stores on the east side and on the west side. And along some stretches, it even has stores in the middle median! My Dad used to tease me all of the time. He said that whenever I had money, that he knew where to find me. Yes, you guessed it: Route 22! Boy, you should have seen me come home with all those bags full of great deals!

My sister, on the other hand, used to shop heavily on a popular TV store. I think that you might know the name: HSN (Home Shopping Network). And they delivered their packages through UPS. Many times I would come home to find our foyer filled with UPS boxes! Dad would hit the roof. He said that he knew when my sister had money –yes, you guessed it- because he saw all of those UPS boxes in our hallway.

Dad would try and chastise my sister and I for making these foolish and wasteful purchases. But, being the true shoppers that we were, my sister and I were resolute in the justification of our purchases. We sharply and confidently retorted, "But Dad, THEY WERE ON SALE! " And I will never forget his response. He wisely said, "It isn't a sale if you don't need it."

Today, many years later, I must admit that Dad was

147

right. For example, let's say that shovels are regularly priced at $20 a piece but are on sale for $1 a piece. This is a great deal, right? Well, that depends. "It depends on what," you may ask. It depends on one thing: whether or not you really need a shovel. If you need a shovel, then you have saved $19. But, if you don't need a shovel, no matter how good the deal, you will waste $1 by purchasing it. Thus, it is wise to purchase only those services and goods that we really need.

c. "Learn To Do Without"

Finally, I am reminded about something that my former barber, Jerome Drayton, shared with me. He told me that when he grew up in the rural South that times were hard. He said that he didn't have many of the luxuries and excesses that today's youth take for granted. Jerry said that on one particular occasion that he kept asking his father for some money. I will never forget the reply that he said his father gave. Jerry said that his father told him, "Son, learn to do without."

This seems like a very harsh statement for a parent to make to their child. However, after years of contemplation, I believe that there is much merit to this statement. I look at my purchases and spending sprees over the years and think, "What if I had learned to do without those things? How much more would I have today?" How much more would you have? However, the most important question now is, "How much will we have?"

Hopefully, we will be able to able to give favorable answers as we "learn to do without."

In summation, it has been suggested that we live within our means. But this chapter suggests an even safer place: living beneath our means. When we live beneath our means, instead of right on the edge, then we put ourselves in a better position to deal with life's unexpected emergencies.

CHAPTER 20
Discernment

"In order to hear people's cries and to wipe away their tears, learn to hear with your eyes and see with your ears."

"We look to the LORD our God for his mercy, just as servants keep their eyes on their master, as a slave girl watches her mistress for the slightest signal."
-Psalm 123:2

In the ancient Far East, Oriental masters seldom spoke to their attendants. Yet, the servants carried out every whim of their masters. This was possible because of the alertness and attentiveness of the servants. They constantly watched their masters for hand signals, facial expressions and hand gestures. This is the situation that the psalmist illustrates in Psalm

123:2. C. H. Spurgeon provides commentary on this verse in *Treasury of David*. He writes:

"[The psalmist] is like a slave standing silent but alert, in the presence of the Oriental "lord", with banns folded on his breast, and eyes fixed on his master, seeking to **read**, and to anticipate, if possible, his every wish. [The psalmist] is like a maiden in attendance on her mistress, anxiously striving to **see** her mind in her looks, to discover and administer to her moods and wants. The grave, reserved Orientals, as we know, seldom speak to their attendants, at least on public occasions. They intimate their wishes and commands by a wave of the hand, by a glance of the eye, by slight movements and gestures which might escape notice, were they not watched for with eager attention. Their slaves "hang upon their faces; "they" fasten their eyes" on the eyes of their master; they watch and obey every turn of his hand, every movement of his finger. Thus the Psalmist conceives of himself as waiting on God, looking to him alone, watching for the faintest signal, bent on catching and obeying it."

Today, this same manner of exchanging information still takes place. It is called 'non-verbal communication.' Everyday people are speaking – without even talking! This chapter addresses two (2) types of non-verbal communication: 1) Auditory: Hearing with our Eyes; and 2) Visual: Seeing with our Ears.

A. Auditory: Hear with Your Eyes

The primary organs for hearing are the ears. However, it is also possible, and many times necessary to "hear with the eyes."

Scuba divers rely on clear communication in order to ensure successful missions. Many times, scuba divers are outfitted with microphones and other equipment to enable dialogue between divers. Also, divers use 'chalkboards' to communicate messages while under water. However, in the event that any of these items malfunction or become unavailable, divers need to be able to communicate with one another. The safeguard for this is the use of underwater hand signals. In an article entitled *Talking Below the Waves*, author Melissa Rodriguez writes:

> "Hand signals remain the most widespread method of underwater communication despite fancy devices that allow you to actually talk with and listen to other divers, providing they have compatible equipment. You could spend big bucks on this type of equipment or indulge in dive slates. For safety purposes, you should still recognize the common hand signals, a form of sign language. You never know when a diver, who doesn't have a communication device other than his or her hands, will try to tell you something urgent like, "I'm out of air!"

Just as there is a sign language for divers, there is the more commonly known sign language for the hearing impaired. This system, commonly known as American Sign Language or ASL, uses hand signals for letters and words. In essence, the eyes serve as 'ears' in that they interpret what a person is saying through the use of sign language.

Body language is another form of non-verbal communication. Whether realized or not, we communicate more with our bodies than we do with our speech. That is, people readily pay more attention to our behavior rather than to our speech. According to A. Barbour, author of *Louder Than Words: Nonverbal Communication*, reports what has the most impact on people listening to a person give a speech. Barbour gives the following breakdown:

- 7 percent verbal (words)

- 38 percent vocal (volume, pitch, rhythm, etc)

- 55 percent body movements (mostly facial expressions)

Realistically, people watch to see if a speaker's actions are complementary and congruent with his/her speech. For example, to say that your product will meet the needs of each client and to shrug your shoulders at the same time could send a mixed message. Posture, eye contact and facial expressions are very important in 'seeing what a person is saying.' Also, gestures, smell and touch communicate a great deal about an individual non-verbally.

Another system of non-verbal communication is employed by law enforcement. This communication system is commonly known as *Talking Hands*. This system allows law enforcement personnel to communicate where normal speech may not be possible. This type of communication is necessary in a noisy environment or when the police don't want the criminals to 'hear' what they are saying. Thus, with 'talking hands,' they are enabled to communicate visually with one another. That is, they are trained to "hear with their eyes' what their partner is saying.

The ability to "hear with our eyes" is vital in identifying the true needs of a person. Many times a person is unwilling and/or unable to verbally express their situation and need. However, if we really pay attention and 'see' instead of look, there are visual cues that tell a person's story.

One of the most prominent visual cues is physical appearance. Much information can be discerned just by looking at a person's appearance. Sometimes, a person that is disheveled and unkempt can be in need of personal assistance. Or a person foraging through a garbage can could be in need of food. Also, lacerations and bruises can indicate physical abuse. It is in these situations that we need to "learn to hear with our eyes."

2. Visual: See with Your Ears

The primary organs responsible for sight are the eyes. Light rays enter through the eye and are converted into electrical signals at the back of the eye. From here, these signals travel along the optic nerve to the brain. Once in the brain, these signals are converted into images. The observation of these images is what we call 'sight.'

However, although the eyes are the primary organs

for seeing, there is another organ that is capable of 'sight.' It is possible, also to 'see with the ears.' This is made evident in nature. Bats -among owls, dolphins and whales- are all capable of 'seeing with their ears.' The scientific term for this capability is *echolocation.* Simply, it is a process of using sound waves to navigate and to locate food. The *Ask Wendell* column by Discovery Communications Inc. provides the following information about the bat and echolocation:

"Those who believe bats are blind just can't see the truth themselves. In reality, all bats can see. Many of them, in fact, can see really well, even in dim light. Most fruit-eating bats, for example, have large bulging eyes that help them find their way and locate food by sight. But other bats, especially those that hunt for insects at night, need to rely a lot more on other senses in the dark. These winged wonders make up for low visibility by "seeing" with their ears, and they do this by using a technique called echolocation. A bat echolocates by sending out streams of high-pitched sounds through its mouth or nose. These signals then bounce off nearby objects and send back echoes. By "reading" these echoes with its super-sensitive ears, the bat can determine the location, distance, size, texture and shape of an object in its environment. In some cases, a bat can even use echoes to tell insects that are edible apart from those that aren't. And even bats which have been blinded can catch their food without a hitch this way."

The super-sensitive ears of the bat enable it to "see with its ears."

This is truly an amazing ability of the bat! But, what about humans: are they able to 'see with their ears?' The answer is, "Yes!"

There is a product on the market that allows a visually-impaired person to 'see.' With the use of a camera, laptop computer and a pair of headphones, a blind person is enabled to see grayscale images of objects around them. This technology appeared in the December 11, 2005 edition of the *New York Times*. Author Alison Motluk writes in her article *Seeing with Your Ears*:

"Seeing is something that most of us expect to do with our eyes. But what if you are born blind or lose your sight later in life? Peter Meijer suggests you consider seeing with your ears instead.

Meijer, a research scientist in the Netherlands, has developed a technology called the vOICe, which allows you to represent visual information - to "see" - with sounds. The device is a tiny camera, a laptop and headphones. The camera is mounted on your head and the laptop takes the video input and converts it into auditory information, or soundscapes. The scene in front of you is scanned in stereo: you hear objects on your left through your left ear and objects on your right through your right ear. Brightness is translated as volume: bright things are louder. Pitch tells you what's up and what's down. The image refreshes once a second.

With practice, Meijer says, you can learn to sense instinctively how the features of a soundscape correspond to objects in the physical world. Pat

157

Fletcher, for instance, a proficient user of the vOICe who could see until age 21, describes the grayscale images in her head as "ghostly" but real. At a meeting of the Cognitive Neuroscience Society in New York in April, researchers from Harvard Medical School announced that when they viewed the activity in the brains of two vOICe users (one blind at birth, the other who went blind later in life), it was in many respects like that of a sighted person while seeing.

Not everyone has the inclination to kit themselves out with a head-mounted camera and a laptop. Fortunately, with the help of an enterprising Bulgarian software company, Meijer has rejiggered his setup to work using one of the most ubiquitous gadgets of our day: the camera phone. Now, after downloading a simplified version of the software, practically anyone can point her camera phone at what she wants to see and have a listen to what it looks like."

Wow! So, technologically, a person can be enabled to 'see with their ears.' But it must be noted that this ability existed in humans way before this wonderful invention.

Jamie Foxx portrayed the late entertainer Ray Charles in the movie *Ray*. In one particular scene of this movie, the character Ray is asked how he is able to go about his daily routine without sight. His response is mind-blowing and captivating! He replies, "I see with my ears." The character Ray wasn't referring to the images that he received through a camera, a laptop computer and headphones when he said this. No, actually he was referring to the ability of all human beings to 'see' their environment by truly 'listening' to the sounds that come from it.

It is amazing what can be heard (i.e. seen) when one actually listens. In another scene in the movie *Ray*, the character Ray and his love interest are seated inside a restaurant. In an effort to woo her, Ray tells his sweetheart that she is like the hummingbird that is hovering outside of the restaurant window. She immediately retorts that there is no hummingbird. The character Ray (Jamie Foxx) then challenges her to 'listen' for it. Then, miraculously and amazingly, she too heard the hummingbird hovering outside of the restaurant window. Its amazing what we can 'see' when we listen for it.

A similar experience appeared in the April 25, 2005 edition of the *Tribune-Review*. In the article *When It Comes to Birdwatching, It's All in the Ears* author Bob Karlovits writes:

"Seeing what your ears tell you is one of the secrets quickly discovered by people new to birding.

"The ears tell more than the eyes," says Patricia O'Neill, the director of education at the Audubon Society's local headquarters at the Beechwood Farms Nature Reserve in Fox Chapel. "Birds are mostly insectivores and they're up at the tops of trees, so when you go on the trail you hear them first."

She says that is an aspect of avian interest that often surprises those at the free "Birding for Beginners" program, which continues Saturday at Beechwood Farms.

David Liebmann, who leads the walks, agrees about the importance of listening. He says he often begins each walk by telling participants to "put their binoculars down and listen to what's around you."

Most people on the bird walks are "used to seeing what's at their birdfeeders," but aren't able to identify the sounds the birds make, he says. He compares it to learning what sounds musical instruments make: You don't know what makes a tuba sound by hearing it alone.

"Once you put a name to it," he says of connecting the bird to the sound, "then you can pick it out."

My Dad, who was served as pastor of our congregation, would often close his eyes while seated in the pulpit. We would often joke that Dad had fallen asleep in service. If he did, it sure would be understandable, considering that he worked three jobs to provide for his family and the church! But on one occasion, Dad revealed his secret. He said, "I know that you all think that I am asleep in the pulpit. And maybe sometimes I am." He then added, "But there is a reason that I keep my eyes closed while in the pulpit. I keep my eyes closed while in the pulpit because I have found out that I can see more with them closed than with them open!" Wow, what wisdom! He explained that he was able to 'see with his ears' what was going in the congregation both spiritually and physically! And this was proven through his revelatory and life-changing messages. His philosophy was this: you have to know where a person is hurting at first before you can help them! Pastor Hansen of the Berea Lutheran Church also supports this view-point. He writes in his message entitled *Seeing with Your Ears*:

"Have you ever tried seeing with your ears? Close your eyes. Just listen. What do you hear? Probably more than you were aware of before closing your eyes.

I want you to [practice] that as a way of discovering something we need to know at Berea. What we need to know is what people who are not practicing Christians are saying that reveals their needs and interests. Close your eyes (at least figuratively). Listen. Listen hard. What concerns, issues and felt needs do you hear your neighbors, co-workers and friends talking about? These are clues that can help us reach out to our community more effectively with events, class offerings and worship experiences that speak to those needs, and we will find a more ready hearing among them.

"Seing with our ears" is not a program. It's a way of life. We...can train ourselves to [listen hard], especially [to] our non-Christian family and friends."

And this is the focus of "seeing with our ears." The truth of the matter is that many people are hurting all around us. And they are trying to tell us this, but many times we don't 'see' (i.e. hear) what they are saying. I don't believe that we do this on purpose. I believe that many of us are so caught up in, just trying to make it through another day, that we inadvertently miss these "cries for help." Thus, we don't hear "the hovering hummingbird." We don't hear the "birds singing." And saddest of all, we can't 'see' that our brother and sister are hurting.

The April 1991 edition of *Bits & Pieces* features some excellent advice on how to truly 'see and hear' what people need. In this article, General George Marshall gives the following advice on 'hearing' what people need. He suggests:

1. "Listen to the other person's story.
2. Listen to the other person's full story.
3. Listen to the other person's full story first."

Therefore, in conclusion, I say, "In order to hear peoples' cries and to wipe away their tears, learn to hear with your eyes and to see with your ears."

CHAPTER 21
Sin

"There is a difference between *committing* a sin
and *continuing* in sin."

*"Those who have been born into God's family do not
sin, because God's life is in them. So they can't keep
on sinning, because they have been born of God."*
I John 3:9

My mother, the late Missionary Mildred E. Roberts, told
me about one of her mission experiences. She took a
bus ride on the bus with a senior missionary partner.
While riding, a gentleman passenger asked a question of this senior missionary. He asked her, "Do Christians sin?" And, according to my mother, the
missionary politely replied, "No, sir. We do not." My
mom said that she was perplexed by this answer.

So, she waited until later and confronted her missionary partner privately. She said to her, "Earlier today, on the bus, you told that gentleman that Christians do not sin." "Yes, that's true, I did tell him that," replied here missionary partner. But, Mom, still being uncomfortable with this answer, probed even further. "But is it true that Christians do not sin," asked my mother. The missionary replied, "Of course, it isn't true. Christians do sin. But I couldn't tell *him* that!"

No doubt about it, the Bible is very clear on God's stance concerning sin. It tells us that, "the wages of sin is death" (Romans 6:23a). For a truth, God warns against it and punishes those that commit it. And it is believed by some that the only persons capable of sinning are unrepentant sinners. It is believed by others that once a person is born again into the family of God that it is impossible to sin anymore. As this chapter shall show, this type of thinking can be damaging and discouraging to believers and unbelievers alike.

When dealing with the topic of sin, I am reminded of pencils and computer keyboards. "What in the world do they have to do with sin?" you may ask. Well, look at a pencil. On one end is pointed graphite for writing symbols on paper. But on the other end is –you guessed right- an eraser. What is it there for? In the event that a mistake is made, it can be erased. Now, look at the computer keyboard. It has a 'delete' key. And, it also has a 'backspace' key. What are they there for? In the event that a mistake is made, it can be erased. In both of these examples, I don't believe that it is the *intent* of humans to make mistakes. However, I do believe that it is in our *nature* to make mistakes. This is what the Apostle Paul expressed in

Romans 7:15-20. He said:

"15 I don't understand myself at all, for I really want to do what is right, but I don't do it. Instead, I do the very thing I hate.

16 I know perfectly well that what I am doing is wrong, and my bad conscience shows that I agree that the law is good.

17 But I can't help myself, because it is sin inside me that makes me do these evil things.

18 I know I am rotten through and through so far as my old sinful nature is concerned. No matter which way I turn, I can't make myself do right. I want to, but I can't.

19 When I want to do good, I don't. And when I try not to do wrong, I do it anyway.

20 But if I am doing what I don't want to do, I am not really the one doing it; the sin within me is doing it."

This nature, or more specifically, sin-nature, is the reason behind many of the mistakes that humans make. However, like pencils and computer keyboards, there is an eraser, a delete key and a backspace key to erase all mistakes (i.e. sins).

This chapter will cover three (3) topics: 1) The Principle of Sin; 2) The Possibility of Sin; and 3) The Provision for Sin.

A. The Principle of Sin

When discussing the origin of sin, it is important and necessary to determine the theatre or venue. When discussing the theatre of heaven, the origin of sin began with Lucifer and the fallen angels during the rebellion (Isaiah 14:12-17; Ezekiel 28:12-19). However, when discussing the theatre of earth, the origin of sin is traced to Adam. Although, his wife Eve was deceived by Satan, it was Adam that transgressed (I Timothy 2:14) God's law (i.e. sinned). And as a result, this sin nature has been passed through genetics on to all subsequent humans. That's right, by just being born, all humans inherit this sin nature. The psalmist speaks of it in Psalm 51:5. He says, "For I was born a sinner—yes, from the moment that my mother conceived me." This process of inheriting the nature of sin from our forefathers is call "The Sin Principle." C. W. Ruth's work *Spiritual Leprosy* mentions the following about the 'sin principle.' It states:

> "LEPROSY HAS long since been recognized as a type of sin; and as leprosy cannot be pardoned, so the principle, sin, cannot be pardoned but has to be treated in a manner similar to that of leprosy-it has to be cleansed.
>
> Leprosy is a type of inbred sin because it is inherited. Sins as transgressions or acts are not transmitted from our parents, but sin as a principle is inherited from our forefathers. This "carnal mind," "the old man," "the law of sin," "the flesh," all refer to this principle of sin. It has come to us by the laws of heredity. It is not the result of an act, but has been born in us as the result of Adam's fall. Hence, I insist leprosy is a type of inbred sin.

166

This principle is born in every child. You see it manifested on every hand. I met a man at one time who argued that the babe did not have this principle of sin and claimed that he didn't have it. I told him I would like to have taken care of him when a baby. There is born in every one of us this principle, which we term inbred sin or the carnal mind. Believe me when I say that there is no child born pure. If the child were born pure, it would have no need of the atonement. You may restrain your child and do your utmost, but despite all of your efforts, when that child comes to the years of accountability it will naturally take to sin...People are never really established until they are sanctified wholly. It makes such a difference when the "old man" and his evil deeds are gone. Destruction of sin in the hearts of believers is a scriptural truth that has been proven in the experience of saints of all ages, including those of today."

Thus, the principle of sin is inherent in all human beings, young and old alike. And it is this principle of sin that leads to the chance of committing a sin. This leads to the second point: *The Possibility of Sin*.

B. The Possibility of Sin

It has been stated in the onset of this chapter that, "*There is a difference between committing a sin and continuing in sin.*" Let me attempt to explain the difference.

1. *Committing a Sin*

Every human being inherits the sin principle simply by the right of birth. And, thus, each human will naturally perform acts against the law of God. However, when an individual is invited by God, unto salvation (John 6:44) and accepts this invitation, they become born again (John 3:3). Once a person experiences this new birth, their mind, body and soul are placed under new management: Jesus Christ. Through governance and guidance by the Holy Spirit, the new believer is able to live a victorious life over sin. This should be the ideal and the goal of every true believer: to live a sin-free life through the power of the Holy Ghost.

However, while the ideal may be to live a sin-free life, the real is that a Christian probably will commit a sin from time to time. This isn't because the person is evil and just wants to sin. One reason has to do with God's high and meticulous demands for holiness and righteousness. Even our best efforts to live daily, sin-free lives can be compared to 'filthy rages.' For it is written in Isaiah 64:6a that:

> "We are all infected and impure with sin. When we proudly display our righteous deeds, we find they are but filthy rags."

Have you ever had the experience of wearing a white outfit and trying to keep it clean throughout the course of the day? Well, I have. And let me tell you, no matter how careful and cautious I am, I get a stain from somewhere. It was my intention to keep it spotless, but in the course of reaching that goal, my outfit was stained.

And, to me, this is much like trying to live a totally right-eous life. In our grandest efforts, some type of sin (e.g. bad thought, bad speech) stains our 'garment.'

Another reason that the possibility to commit a sin exists with Christians is this: at the time of salvation and conversion all parts of the individual are not redeemed. In short, some parts of a person's being are immediately delivered from the power of sin while others are not. A story about the city of Chicago illustrates this point. In the early 20th century, the mayor of Chicago had rid-den the city of all crime and corruption –well, almost everywhere in the city. You see, although the major portion of the city was crime-free, certain portions well still controlled by the mafia. This parallels the life of the born-again believer. There are parts of their personality and soul that are saved, however there are still parts that are awaiting redemption. I experienced this first-hand during my reclaiming. At the time, I was partying at clubs and using profanity. The Spirit of Jesus Christ met me in the club one night and asked me if I was ready to do His will. I said, "Yes" and left the club that night a changed man! Hallelujah! Two things 'fell off' immediately upon my conversion: 1) I stopped partying at clubs; and 2) I stopped using profane language. However, to date, there are certain sins that didn't 'fall off' during my conversion. I still struggle with them to-day. Two of them are: 1) Fear; and 2) Doubt. And if you don't think that these are big sins, then check out Revelation 21:8. It says:

"But the fearful, and unbelieving, and the abomi-nable, and murderers, and whoremongers, and sorcerers, and idolaters, and all liars, shall have their part in the lake which burneth with fire and brimstone: which is the second death."

However, despite my inadequacies, I am yet confident that Jesus Christ will make me a conqueror over these things as I continue to submit to His will and accept His help. Perhaps, this is the why the Apostle Paul gave this encouragement in Philippians 1:6:

> "And I am sure that God, who began the good work within you, will continue his work until it is finally finished on that day when Christ Jesus comes back again."

I am totally convinced that it will ultimately take the power of Jesus Christ through His Holy Spirit to totally deliver us from the bondage of sin!

2. Continuing in Sin

On the other hand, while it is possible for a believer to commit a sin, it is impossible for them to continue in sin. A believer can make a mistake, but as soon as he or she does, they are truly sorry for their action and will repent. However, it is impossible for a believer to continue in sin. In other words, it is impossible for that person to continually live a life of sin and have a clear conscience towards God.

Imagine this, you and I are sitting at a table enjoying a delicious meal together. Then, by mistake, I accidentally kick your leg under the table. You holler and I apologize. Then, after the first apology, I kick your leg again...and again...and again! There is no way that I can truly be sorry –or your friend for that matter- to continually and knowingly cause you harm. This is the same thing that happens when a person continually sins against God. They continually hurt Him while 'claiming' that they are sorry. Likewise, it is impossible for a believer to continue in a life of sin.

In regards to living a life of sin, W. E. Best writes in *A Greatly Misunderstood Passage of Scripture*:

> "There are acts of sin in every Christian, but there can never be a life of sin. The person born of God practices righteousness, but the person not born of God practices sin, because he is of the devil.
>
> The person who "does not practice sin" and "cannot sin" manifest two parts of a whole (I John 3:9). The first is an assertion of a fact, and the second is a principle which explains and confirms the fact. To live a life of sin is contrary to God's giving the principle of life. It has been said, "The heavenly life breeds birds of paradise." John does not deny the fact that Christians sin (I John 1:6-2:1), but they are not confirmed sinners. The character of true believers in Christ is revealed in I John 3:7—"Little children, let no one deceive you; the one who practices righteousness is righteous, just as He is righteous" (NASB). They do not sin as they did before they were born of the Spirit (John 3:8). "

Thus, once a person is truly born again, they will not be able to "continue in sin." This leads to the third and final point: *The Provision for Sin.*

3. The Provision for Sin

Thus, it has been established that the possibility always exists for believers to sin. This is supported by the Apostle John's statement in I John 2:1 where he states, "If anyone sins…" However, this isn't an excuse or a time to pet sin, but to confess and uncover it! The possibility to sin in no way decimates God's holiness and intolerance for sin! It must be dealt with swiftly and effectively.

But who is qualified to erase and absolve sin? The answer to this is simple: Jesus Christ through His Blood. The Apostle John tells us that Jesus is the Provision for the believer's sin. He further states in I John 2:1,2:

>   1. "My little children, these things write I unto you, that ye sin not. And if any man sin, we have an advocate with the Father, Jesus Christ the righteous:
>   2. And he is the propitiation for our sins: and not for ours only, but also for the sins of the whole world. "

W. E. Best writes in *A Greatly Misunderstood Passage of Scripture*:

> "There is always the possibility of children sinning— "if anyone sins" (I John 2:1 NASB). We must not only resolve not to sin, but we must able to recognize when we sin. This presents despair when we do sin. The committed sin can never be covered or excused by man. To imagine that God would excuse sin which is against eternal law is to turn His

justice into iniquity. God's covering of sin includes its unveiling. Confession involves forsaking. Therefore, our covering must be preceded by God's covering. Many religionists talk and act like they are more forgiving than God.

The provision for the believer's sin is stated: "...we have an Advocate" (parakletos, meaning one who pleads the cause of another, or sent to assist another—used in John 14:16, 26; 15:26; 16:7; I John 2:1). The believer's sin offends the Father, and the term "Father" denotes relationship. As Priest, Christ deals with the guilt of sin. As Advocate, He restores the sinning soul to fellowship. The efficacy of His action is guaranteed by the righteousness of His Person and the value of His propitiation. Before Peter sinned, Christ prayed for Him; when he sinned, Christ looked on him and restored him. Not only did Christ restore Peter, but He used him.

Sin can never be covered permanently or excused by man. To imagine that God would excuse sin which is against His eternal law is to turn His justice into iniquity and His wisdom into unrighteousness. God's covering of sin includes its unveiling. Confession includes forsaking. Our covering must be preceded by God's covering."

We have discussed much concerning sin in this chapter and I therefore feel led by the Spirit to invite you to an 'altar call." By altar call, it is meant that this is a time to speak to Jesus Christ for yourself and accept Him as your Lord and Savior. "But, I am not at an altar," you might be thinking. Well, let me share something with you that I learned from a prominent man of God. It was during one of the semi-annual convocations and the church was packed. At one point during the service, Bishop Norman Prescott of the Church of God In Christ made an altar call. Usually, everyone would gather around the area at the base of the pulpit. However, there were too many people to do this. It was then that Bishop Prescott shared some profound knowledge with the congregation. He said, "Normally, I would call you up to the altar. But, tonight I'm not going to do that." He added, "I'm not going to call you up to the altar tonight, because I want you to learn something. I want you to know that wherever you are standing at tonight is your altar!" Bishop Prescott gave the prayer and souls were blessed!

And that is what I want you to know. Wherever you are right now –in your bedroom, bathroom, car, office- is your altar. It is simply the place where you meet and speak with God. The patriarchs, Abraham, Jacob and Moses, didn't have the luxury of meeting God in air-conditioned, carpeted auditoriums. No they met God in the desert and built altars out of what they could find, usually stones. These altars served as perennial testaments that God had met with a human being in the earth.

I don't care what your sin is or what your sins are, the blood of Jesus is ready to wash them all away right know. It is written in His word in Isaiah 1:18:

"Come now, and let us reason together, saith the LORD: though your **sins** be as **scarlet**, they shall be as white as snow; though they be red like crimson, they shall be as wool."

Are you ready? If you want Jesus to forgive your sins and accept you as His own then pray these words:

Lord Jesus, I come to you as humbly as I know how.

And I thank you for every blessing that you have bestowed upon me.

I acknowledge that you are the only true and living God.

I acknowledge that I am a sinner and I am sorry for all of my sins.

Please forgive me and cleanse me from all unrighteousness.

I believe that you died for my sins and the sins of the entire world.

I believe that you rose on the third day, ascended into Heaven and are seated at the right hand of the Father.

I believe that you will return to judge those who are alive and those who are dead.

I confess you Jesus with my mouth and believe in my heart that you are the Christ.

By faith through grace, I AM SAVED!

Thank you, Jesus!

If you believe what you have just said, then you are saved, my friend! Welcome to the Family! And according to scripture, there is a big party going on in Heaven right now in honor of your conversion! For it is written in Luke 15:10:

> "…[There] is joy in the presence of God's angels when even one sinner repents."

I recommend now, that through prayer, you seek out a Bible-believing, Bible-teaching ministry in your area. This will allow you to gain further instruction about your new life and to mature in Jesus Christ! If I can be of any assistance in this area, please feel free to write me at the address provided.

Thank you so much for supporting my ministry and may God continually bless you with *Effective Living*."

Amen.

www.ingramcontent.com/pod-product-compliance
Lightning Source LLC
Chambersburg PA
CBHW031257090426
42742CB00007B/500